GLOBAL ORGANIZATIONS

The Organization
of American States

GLOBAL ORGANIZATIONS

The African Union

The Arab League

The Association of Southeast Asian Nations

The Caribbean Community and Common Market

The European Union

The International Atomic Energy Agency

The Organization of American States

The Organization of Petroleum
Exporting Countries

The United Nations

The United Nations Children's Fund

The World Bank and
the International Monetary Fund

The World Health Organization

The World Trade Organization

GLOBAL ORGANIZATIONS

The Organization of American States

Barbara Lee Bloom

Series Editor
Peggy Kahn
University of Michigan–Flint

CHELSEA HOUSE
PUBLISHERS
An imprint of Infobase Publishing

The Organization of American States
Copyright © 2008 by Infobase Publishing

Chelsea House
An imprint of Infobase Publishing
132 West 31st Street
New York NY 10001

Library of Congress Cataloging-in-Publication Data
Bloom, Barbara Lee, 1943–
  Organization of American States / Barbara Lee Bloom.
    p. cm. — (Global organizations)
  ISBN: 978-0-7910-9544-7 (hardcover)
  1. Organization of American States. I. Title. II. Series.

  JZ5331.5.OB56 2008
  341.24'5—dc22   2007042652

Series design by Erik Lindstrom
Cover design by Ben Peterson

Printed in the United States of America

Bang KT 10 9 8 7 6 5 4 3 2 1

This book is printed on acid-free paper.

All links and Web addresses were checked and verified to be correct at the time of publication. Because of the dynamic nature of the Web, some addresses and links may have changed since publication and may no longer be valid.

CONTENTS

INTRODUCTION

Land Mines in the Americas

In Nicaragua, in 1990, nine-year-old José García ran through the pasture with his cousin gathering their family's livestock. Suddenly a land mine hidden underground exploded, tearing off José's left leg and killing his cousin. José lived in an area that had been mined by Nicaraguans to fight against the U.S.-backed Contra (Spanish abbreviation for "counterrevolutionary") guerrillas. Seventeen years later, José, who has learned to live with one leg, says, "The war is over here, but the consequences of it are still here."[1]

At a hospital in Nicaragua's capital city, Managua, lay 15-year-old Edwin Cornejo. He lost most of his sight and both of his arms in January 2005, when he picked up what turned out to be a mine detonator, left by a former renter, in his home in San Juan de Rio Coco, a village in Nicaragua. His mother, Luisa, stood at his bedside, "He doesn't know he's lost his arms," she told visitors. "He keeps asking what's wrong with his face…. I tell him just a few bumps and scratches, my dear." Luisa explained how she had rented out the room for extra money. "I just don't understand how that thing got into the house. It's ruined my baby. Why would someone leave something like that behind?" Hovering over her son, Luisa tried to comfort Edwin as he winced in pain. "I didn't know that dangerous thing was there," she said. "Dear God Almighty, how will I manage to take care of him?"[2]

Although a peace agreement officially ended the civil war in Nicaragua in 1990, the horrors associated with land mines continue. During the conflict between government and Contra guerrilla forces from 1979 to 1990, neighboring Honduras and Costa Rica also had land mines hidden along their borders. Most of the mines used during the fighting in Central America were buried in the jungles and thick growth around the camps where the Contras hid during the war. The small devices proved hard to find after the fighting stopped. Even with old army maps and information from those living in the areas, it remains difficult to clear minefields. In the rain forests and along mountainsides, heavy rains often bring mudslides and move mines to new locations.

Other conflicts in South America have left hundreds of thousands of land mines unexploded. Suriname has thousands of mines left from a guerrilla war in the 1980s. Chile's long border with Argentina, Peru, and Bolivia has more than 100,000 mines, buried during border disputes. From a conflict between Peru and Ecuador, more land mines stay hidden. In Colombia, it is estimated that about 50,000 mines have been planted by guerrillas. Nonetheless, Nicaragua is the country where the most land mines were buried, and its citizens have experienced the most death and injuries.

Concern over these horrifying weapons led five Central American countries—Nicaragua, El Salvador, Guatemala,

In the early 1990s, Nicaragua was considered one of the most mine-affected nations in Central America. During Nicaragua's civil war, more than 135,000 land mines were planted, with the northern border it shares with Honduras being the most heavily impacted. Since 1990, the year the war ended, 82 people have been killed and 905 injured. In 2002, Costa Rica declared itself mine safe, and Nicaragua is working toward becoming the next land-mine free nation in the region.

Honduras, and Costa Rica—to ask for help removing them. Their government leaders requested assistance from the Organization of American States (OAS), the largest inter-American association of nations in the Western Hemisphere. The OAS responded and passed several resolutions. It created the Assistance Program for De-mining in Central America, and before long, the program grew to include plans for all countries in the hemisphere. Now called the Mine Action Program, its goal is to clear away all land mines in the Western Hemisphere.

The OAS, through one of its partner organizations—the Inter-American Defense Board—created de-mining teams to clear the mines from the countries where they remained. International experts trained local police and soldiers to find and remove the mines in the field. For example, two military officers from Honduras supervised 28 Colombian army and navy officers who found and removed mines in 30 fields. Soldiers de-mining a field first rope off the area and then use metal detectors and long rods to locate the mines. With great care, they dig them up and disarm them. After a border dispute between Peru and Ecuador ended, the OAS trained Peruvian police, who subsequently destroyed more than 20,000 mines located around 415 electric towers in the Condor Mountain Range. In Ecuador, monitoring teams were also trained in removal techniques. Some of the money came from the European Commission. In Nicaragua, the European Commission along with the United States, Canada, Sweden, Norway, and Italy supported the OAS land-mine projects.

In addition to explosive devices hidden in the ground, some countries have stores of land mines on hand. Ongoing border disputes have encouraged some Latin American countries to keep mines ready to use. But the OAS is trying to clear such stockpiles from the hemisphere. Since 1999, more than one million stockpiled mines have been demolished by the OAS. In one of the biggest operations in 2004, Colombia destroyed almost 7,000 from its supply.

The OAS Mine Action Program realized that removal of stockpiles and mines was only part of the problem. It also addressed other major concerns including assisting victims, supporting a ban on all such devices in the hemisphere, and educating the local population to minimize risk. The education projects teach civilians in areas where mines are known to exist how to avoid them. Educators meet with local people to discuss safe practices such as using roads and paths whenever possible to lessen the threat of death or injuries. The OAS provides charts and photos to school-age children showing what the devices look like so they can avoid them and notify adults. Many of the land-mine victims are children. Colombia has more than 500 victims under age 16.

Beginning in 1997, the program started offering help to those injured in Nicaragua. Now, victims, like José and Edwin, can get medical help, prostheses (artificial limbs), food, housing, and in some cases training to learn new trades. Often the explosions cause blindness in children, as in the case of Edwin Cornejo. Those who lose their eyesight have more than just physical problems. Blindness changes life forever, and children must relearn the skills of simple living. With the aid of international donors, the OAS is able to provide a few children with help at a Costa Rican center, teaching new ways to live independently without sight. William McDonough, director of the OAS Mine Action Program, says, "Vision treatment is essential to restoring not only victim's confidence but also a way to restore their lost childhood."[3]

Adults also lose limbs to land mines. They, too, have to find new ways to live in society. The OAS projects include training adults with new skills so they can earn money. Francisco Peralta was a soldier in the war in Nicaragua when a land mine blew off his left leg and arm. In a recent OAS training program, Peralta learned carpentry skills. With his new trade, he hopes to contribute to the support of his family. Having a trade is vitally important in a country where poverty means many people live in shacks without electricity or running water. So far the program has provided job training to more than 200 land-mine survivors. In Colombia, where national statistics report an average of 2.5 mine accidents each day, this seems quite small. But for a few individuals, it has brought some hope.

While the war was still going on in Nicaragua, a U.S. teacher named Jody Williams became concerned for the safety of the peoples of Central America. She began to work for an organization to bring humanitarian aid to the war-torn region.

She believed more was needed to help, so in 1992, Williams organized the International Campaign to Ban Landmines (ICBL). She traveled around the world speaking and teaching about the problem of antipersonnel land mines, which are designed to kill people. She wanted to make the problem known to the world.

In part because of Williams's efforts, at an international meeting in Ottawa, Canada, in December 1997, 122 countries signed a treaty to ban antipersonnel land mines. Called the Ottawa Convention, this treaty calls for "a total ban on the production, sale, transfer and use of antipersonnel land mines in the region." Although the OAS has asked all states in the hemisphere to ratify or have their governments agree to follow the laws of the treaty, the United States and Cuba so far have failed to do so. As a result of Williams's work, she and ICBL shared the 1997 Nobel Peace Prize.

While there is still much work to be done to save the hemisphere from the scourge of land mines, progress is being made. On December 10, 2002, Costa Rica declared itself free from antipersonnel land mines. A member of the OAS, Costa Rica signed the Ottawa Convention in 1997, and its government ratified it in 1999. Thus, Costa Rica offers hope for the future elimination of land mines and their use in the Western Hemisphere.

The Americas and the Organization of American States

THE ORGANIZATION OF AMERICAN STATES (OAS) IS THE oldest and largest association of nations in the Western Hemisphere. Today, it is a union involving 35 American states. Although people living in the United States often call themselves Americans, people in Chile, Peru, Mexico, Panama, and most countries in the hemisphere also call themselves Americans. This hemisphere, after all, is made up of North, Central, and South America, as well as the Caribbean.

The Americas stretch from the icy shores of northern Canada to the chilly seas around Punto Toro, Chile, the world's most southern town. The 9 million square miles (14.48 million square kilometers) of Latin America are larger than the 7.4 million square miles (11.9 million square kilometers) of Canada and the United States put together. Modern world maps show more accurately the size of the Southern Hemisphere than maps of the past. Bounded by the Pacific Ocean on the west and the Atlantic on the east, the southern part of the continent is divided by the snow-capped Andes. In the spring, the melting snows feed several mighty rivers in South America, including the Amazon, which holds 20 percent of the world's freshwater. The Amazon region contains the world's largest rain forest and some of the world's greatest biodiversity of plants and animals. Though less high than the Andes, a mountain chain continues through Central America into the northern latitudes, forming the Rocky Mountains of the United States and the Canadian Rockies. The Caribbean region is a series of islands reaching more than 2,500 miles from just off the Atlantic coast of South America and curving toward Central America and on to southern Mexico. This region contains miles of sandy beaches, where the Caribbean Sea washes the shores, but here, too, mountains stretch up from the coast.

THE AMERICAS AND THE AMERICANS

Despite so many people calling themselves Americans, the historical backgrounds of South and Central American and Caribbean peoples differ greatly from those living in North America. Most of the United States' southern neighbors remained part of a colonial empire longer than the United States. The majority were Spanish colonies, though Brazil was Portuguese and a few were French, Dutch, or British. The kings and queens of Europe wanted riches from the New World. Spanish conquistadors and other adventurers were only too eager to come to the New World to seek their fame or fortune. Gold, silver, copper, and other minerals first drew the Europeans; later, agricultural products brought wealth to the newcomers. These early colonists frequently enslaved the indigenous peoples or brought slaves from Africa to work their mines and harvest their crops. While most Native Americans fought to remain free, European diseases or superior weapons killed hundreds of thousands of them. Some of those who survived intermarried with the Europeans, and they usually achieved a higher place in the society because they were racially mixed, or known as mestizos. Those of mixed African and European descent were called mulattoes. People with wealth and power tried to copy European lifestyles, while those at the bottom of the society tried to survive.

In the early 1800s, several Latin American countries fought for and won their independence from Spain. Eventually, most colonies freed themselves from European rule and established new governments. Many Caribbean countries, though, failed to gain independence until after World War II, and a few areas, such as the U.S. Virgin Islands, still are territories, belonging to the United States, the United Kingdom (England), the Dutch, or France. Because some countries remained colonies for so many years, their governments and their trade and industries continued to be dependent on Europe. Many countries provided agricultural products, such as coffee, sugar, and tropical fruits, or minerals and metals to the United States and Europe.

Today, a half billion people live in the southern part of the Western Hemisphere, and Latin America and the Caribbean are changing rapidly. No longer are they the rural societies they once were, for most of their people now live in cities. Latin America, though, has the most unequal living standards of any place in the world. A few rich and elite individuals have more of the wealth and own more of the land than in any other region of the world. This gap has created problems for those living in these countries; the majority of the people still struggle to make a decent wage and to live with dignity in their societies. As a result, citizens often take matters into their own hands, not waiting for their governments to help. For example, poor parents living in shacks built on the desert hills of Trujillo, Peru, cleared old dumping grounds so their children had places to play. They also worked with a nongovernmental organization, which sent volunteers to teach their children. People tried to overthrow dictators and set up new governments.

Americans represent ethnically diverse peoples living in different environments, with differing histories, cultures, and traditions. They are part of sovereign states or countries that are free from outside control. During the first century of their independence, these sovereign countries created modern-day states, with constitutions and laws. Although the states of Latin America and the Caribbean valued self-rule, they also wanted to form alliances. They believed together they could improve their country by cooperating on trade, business, legal matters, communications, education, technology, and other common interests.

THE ORGANIZATION OF AMERICAN STATES: A NEW ALLIANCE

The end of World War II forced the global community to realize the world was changing, and countries needed to find different ways to connect with each other. Some new organizations were needed. Threats to international peace and even civilized society required greater cooperation among states. Even before the end of World War II, though, most sovereign countries in the Western Hemisphere had signed multilateral, or more than two-state, agreements. As World War II ended, a peaceful world and security from intervention by other countries were major goals. Americans and everyone else wanted to find ways to stop the spread of wars. The United Nations (UN) was established as a global organization to make the world safe from future wars. When the UN charter was written, it allowed regional organizations to settle local conflicts and work together for protection from warring states.

The leaders of Latin America and the United States decided they wanted an alliance of the Western Hemisphere.

The OAS's Rio Treaty, here being signed by Cuban President Carlos Socarras, was created to provide defense and assistance for OAS members facing an armed attack. While the United States viewed the OAS as a device to protect Latin American countries from Communism during the Cold War, Latin America stressed the organization's role in supporting economic development efforts.

Diplomats worked for several months on a charter for a new organization. Finally, with the approval of the United Nations, the Organization of American States became the first regional organization established after World War II. It was an historic moment in Pan-American relations when 21 American nations signed the charter of the Organization of American States. As Christopher R. Thomas, from Barbados and a future assistant secretary-general to the OAS, later wrote:

For the first time the future preservation of humanity became a pressing issue. . . . Circumstances were
therefore both cogent [convincing] and compelling for
the development of a vision of a Western Hemisphere
united in peace, prosperity and co-operation—a vision
that would carve a hemispheric identity vis-à-vis the
rest of the world. Indeed, the promulgation [putting
into operation] of the Charter of the Organization of
American States in 1948, constituted the maturing outgrowth of a progressive hemispheric vision at a time of
growing anxieties for the future of peace and security
of the region as a whole.[4]

THE GOALS OF THE OAS

The charter's primary objective was to protect the Western
Hemisphere from conflict. The original charter stated, "An act
of aggression against one American State is an act of aggression against all the other American States."[5] The OAS charter
also called for each nation to have the right to determine its
own form of government, without the intervention of any
other state into its affairs. In addition, it condemned wars to
take over another country, saying victory does not bring rights
to the winner.

In the years after the war, hopes for keeping peace ran high.
Many of the goals set out in the original charter represented
ideals to work toward, but the charter never listed how to put
them into operation. Over time, both the Western Hemisphere
and the world changed, and the concerns of the countries
changed as well. For this reason, the original charter has been
amended many times, but the original goals and purposes
have remained much the same. As threats of outside intervention decreased, more emphasis has been placed on raising the
low standards of living in the hemisphere. From the 1970s to

the 1990s, several states with dictatorships or military regimes had revolutions, and citizens tried to establish democratic governments. The OAS responded by deepening its commitment to democracy. In stressing democratic government, the OAS also began to work for human rights. These include economic and social rights, such as the right to live without hunger, as well as political and civil rights, such as the right to vote. Citizenship brings the right to live with protection from extreme poverty as much as from military attack. As a result, goals to improve democracy and raise living standards for all people have been added to the original purposes. Article 2 of the OAS charter now states:

> The Organization of American States, in order to put into practice the principles on which it is founded and to fulfill its regional obligations under the Charter of the United Nations, proclaims the following essential purposes:
>
> a) To strengthen the peace and security of the continent;
>
> b) To promote and consolidate representative democracy, with due respect for the principle of non-intervention;
>
> c) To prevent possible causes of difficulties and to ensure the pacific [peaceful] settlement of disputes that may arise among the Member States;
>
> d) To provide for common action on the part of those States in the event of aggression;
>
> e) To seek the solution of political, juridical, and economic problems that may arise among them;
>
> f) To promote by cooperative action, their economic, social, and cultural development;
>
> g) To eradicate extreme poverty, which constitutes an obstacle to the full democratic development of the peoples of the hemisphere; and

h) To achieve an effective limitation of conventional weapons that will make it possible to devote the largest amount of resources to the economic and social development of the Member States.[6]

MEMBERSHIP IN THE OAS

Twenty-one countries signed the OAS charter in 1948, and by 1951, two-thirds of the governments had ratified or agreed to it, making it international law. The voting process in the OAS gives each nation one vote, with most decisions requiring only a majority. Unlike in the United Nations, there is no veto. Important decisions, such as forming a new agency or changing the charter, require a two-thirds majority. Once two-thirds of the member states ratify a resolution, it becomes international law.

In the years since its founding, the OAS has increased from 21 to 35 member states. Even though all independent states of the Western Hemisphere are eligible for membership, colonies and territories such as French Guiana and the U.S. Virgin Islands are excluded. The majority of new members have come from the ex-colonies of the Caribbean, which gained independence after World War II. Barbados and Trinidad and Tobago became the first of the former colonies to join in 1967. The newest members are Belize and Guyana, which joined the OAS in 1991. Canada became a member in 1990, realizing the importance of an alliance with its southern neighbors. From the beginning, the OAS has conducted its business in the four languages of its members: French, English, Portuguese, and Spanish.

The original charter made no provisions for the exclusion of any member. During the 1960s, though, when the United States feared international Communism and desperately wanted to stop its spread to the hemisphere, its representative to the OAS introduced a resolution to expel Cuba. The resolution said that

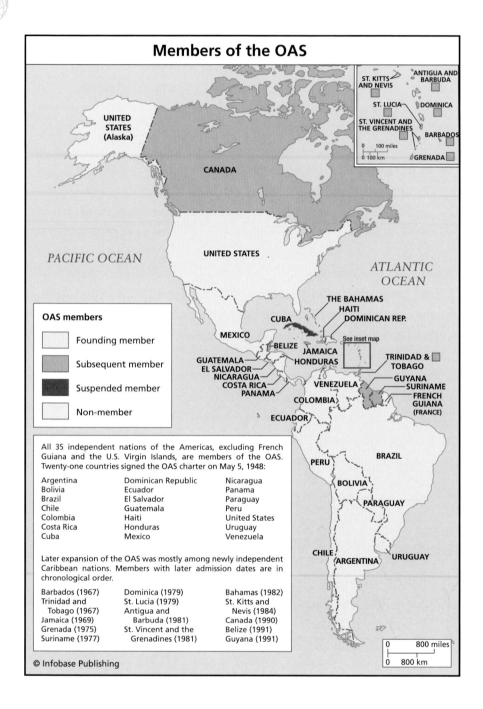

Members of the OAS

ANTIGUA AND BARBUDA
ST. KITTS AND NEVIS
ST. LUCIA — DOMINICA
ST. VINCENT AND THE GRENADINES
BARBADOS
0   100 miles
0 100 km   GRENADA

UNITED STATES (Alaska)

CANADA

PACIFIC OCEAN

UNITED STATES

ATLANTIC OCEAN

THE BAHAMAS
HAITI
CUBA   DOMINICAN REP.
MEXICO
BELIZE
JAMAICA   See inset map
GUATEMALA   HONDURAS   TRINIDAD & TOBAGO
EL SALVADOR
NICARAGUA   GUYANA
COSTA RICA   VENEZUELA   SURINAME
PANAMA   FRENCH GUIANA (FRANCE)
COLOMBIA
ECUADOR

PERU   BRAZIL

BOLIVIA

PARAGUAY

CHILE   ARGENTINA   URUGUAY

OAS members

- ☐ Founding member
- ☐ Subsequent member
- ☐ Suspended member
- ☐ Non-member

All 35 independent nations of the Americas, excluding French Guiana and the U.S. Virgin Islands, are members of the OAS. Twenty-one countries signed the OAS charter on May 5, 1948:

Argentina	Dominican Republic	Nicaragua
Bolivia	Ecuador	Panama
Brazil	El Salvador	Paraguay
Chile	Guatemala	Peru
Colombia	Haiti	United States
Costa Rica	Honduras	Uruguay
Cuba	Mexico	Venezuela

Later expansion of the OAS was mostly among newly independent Caribbean nations. Members with later admission dates are in chronological order.

Barbados (1967)	Dominica (1979)	Bahamas (1982)
Trinidad and Tobago (1967)	St. Lucia (1979)	St. Kitts and Nevis (1984)
Jamaica (1969)	Antigua and Barbuda (1981)	Canada (1990)
Grenada (1975)	St. Vincent and the Grenadines (1981)	Belize (1991)
Suriname (1977)		Guyana (1991)

0   800 miles
0   800 km

© Infobase Publishing

because Cuba was a Communist government, with national ownership of industries and only one political party, it was unsuited to the goals of the OAS and should be excluded. Cuba voted no, six countries abstained, and 14 member states voted yes, and so it met the two-thirds majority needed for this type of resolution. Cuba was excluded from the OAS in January 1962. In October, the Soviet Union sent ships with missiles toward Cuba. The OAS agreed to a naval embargo, or blockage, of all weapons going into the country. As Soviet ships approached Cuba, they met vessels from the United States, Venezuela, and Argentina. The goal was to stop these missiles from entering Cuban waters. Many Americans feared a battle at sea. In the end, the Soviet transports turned back and avoided a conflict.

In 1975, at a meeting in Costa Rica, the OAS withdrew its embargo. Since then, various countries have brought up the idea of restoring Cuba's active membership to the OAS, but the United States continues to oppose it. Other member countries, though, have returned to normal relations with Cuba outside the OAS. Thus, Cuba is still officially a member state, but it is denied participation. Its leaders say it no longer wants membership.

PERMANENT OBSERVERS

Because of the growing interest of the global community in Latin America, the OAS decided in 1972 to allow nonmember countries to send permanent observers. Today, 60 permanent observers from the European Union and from countries around the world attend OAS meetings and activities. As nonvoting observers and speakers, they cooperate on projects with the OAS, providing funds, specialized services, training courses, expert advice, and equipment. For example, the European Union, Sweden, Norway, and Italy—as well as OAS members the United States and Canada—gave money and in-kind contributions, such as trucks and ambulances, to the Mine Action Program coordinated by the OAS. In 2006, the OAS reported:

In the past seven years, the Organization has received the equivalent of US$6.9 million in contributions in kind from Spain, Israel, Korea, France, Russia, Italy, Romania, and Thailand, primarily in training scholarships and in the form of equipment, computers, and vehicles.[7]

THE OAS WORKS IN MANY WAYS

The OAS works to fulfill its principles through a broad network of interconnected agencies, conferences, councils, committees, commissions, and institutions. Much of the actual work of the OAS, from helping women gain fair wages to immunizing against polio, is done through its many agencies and partner institutions. These widely differing agencies of the OAS operate in each member state in the hemisphere. They cooperate with local and national governments, as well as with individuals, schools, churches, nongovernmental organizations, and local and private organizations. They work on areas as different as education, technology, health care, agriculture, legal systems, human rights, drug eradication, and terrorism. Programs and projects are set up to solve concerns of member states. One example is the Mine Action Program.

Over the years, the OAS has adapted its activities as well as its major decision-making bodies to fit changing conditions in the global community and the Western Hemisphere. Some decision-making bodies, like the secretary-general's office, have gained more authority and importance. In transforming itself, the OAS has accepted new ideas and established different procedures. It has added new commissions such as the Inter-American Nuclear Energy Commission. The OAS no longer fears foreign attacks by European powers. Today, it concentrates on spreading democratic governments, and many institutions work on improving economic growth or the well-being of the peoples of the region.

From the beginning, though, Western Hemisphere countries have held different ideas about how best to achieve the OAS aims. Latin American countries wanted to bring peace and eliminate widespread poverty with aid and technical help from the United States to build their industries and businesses.

The U.S. government, instead, supported U.S. corporations in Latin America rather than helping establish independent American businesses. Many citizens and officials of American states accused the OAS of being a tool of U.S foreign policy and imperialism, trying to gain political, economic, or cultural control over their countries. For example, the United States CIA led an invasion of Guatemala in 1954, overthrowing President Jacobo Árbenz Guzmán and restoring U.S. economic and political dominance to Guatemala. The Guatemalan president had tried to eliminate a monopoly held by United Fruit Company, a U.S. corporation. U.S. leaders claimed the Árbenz government was communistic. Latin Americans saw Árbenz's policies as necessary social and economic reform. In the OAS, U.S. Secretary of State John Foster Dulles called for solidarity against Communism. With great U.S. pressure, the OAS defined international Communism as a threat to hemispheric peace, which then justified intervention. At the same time, the United States failed to answer Latin Americans' plea for major economic aid to help the peoples of the region. Thus, many Latin Americans believed the United States used the OAS to expand its own influence and power at the expense of its southern neighbors. Although the charter grants equality among the members, there is little doubt that until recently the United States and its wishes have prevailed.

THE OAS ADJUSTS TO NEW CONDITIONS

Since its founding, the OAS has passed through various stages. It began after World War II as an alliance concerned mainly with peace and the settlement of conflicts. It continues in the twenty-first century as a forum to discuss various hemispheric concerns. From the beginning, Latin American leaders have stressed the importance of improving standards for living as a way to bring peace, democracy, and security to the region. Explaining this view, Carlos Andrés Pérez, president of Venezuela, said in 1990: "Peoples and leaders have become convinced that without economic growth and development, political freedom will remain fragile."[8]

The OAS has existed more than half a century, and during that time, it has transformed itself in an effort to meet the needs of a changing global community. The roots of the OAS, though, go back more than 200 years.

Early History of the OAS

In the early years of the nineteenth century, Simón Bolívar, a wealthy landowner of the New World, led armies against the Spanish crown. By 1824, he had eliminated Spanish rule from the Americas. He believed that if the ex-colonies were to remain independent, they needed some sort of federation to protect their freedom. In 1826, he invited each newly independent country of Spanish-America, as well as the United States, to come to a conference in Panama to discuss a possible alliance of American states. For all delegates, the trip was long and difficult, and the U.S. representative even died along the way. Only Gran Colombia (which included present-day Colombia, Ecuador, Panama, and Venezuela), Peru, Mexico, and Central America sent representatives. At this meeting, called the Congress of

(continues on page 28)

SIMÓN BOLÍVAR, THE LIBERATOR

Few people have had a country named after them, but Simón Bolívar did. He was born in 1783 in Caracas, Venezuela, a Spanish colony, and raised in a house filled with servants. From his tutor, Bolívar learned about the democracies of the Roman and Greek empires. His parents died when he was nine years old, and he lived with his uncle. When he was 21 years old, he went to Europe and saw Napoleon Bonaparte grab the title of emperor, betraying the democratic ideals of the French Revolution.

Soon after, he returned home and joined patriots who overthrew the Spanish viceroy. In 1810, they declared Venezuelan independence. For the new government, Bolívar wrote the Cartagena Manifesto, calling for a strong central government.

Later, Bolívar put together an army and set out to liberate the Americas. After many battles and defeats, in 1821, his armies triumphed, and he organized the Republic of Gran Colombia, including Venezuela, Colombia, Panama, and Ecuador. He became the first president. In 1824, Bolívar marched into Peru, and eventually, he ended Spain's rule in South America. A year later, Upper Peru separated, took the name Bolivia to honor him, and declared him president for life.

Bolívar longed to keep the Americas independent from Europe, and he dreamed of a lasting alliance of American republics. He organized the Congress of Panama in 1826. This was the first hemispheric conference, but governments failed to support a federation.

By 1830, opposition formed against Bolívar's government in Gran Colombia. Shortly afterward, Bolívar resigned as president. He died resentful of the ingratitude for his efforts. Today, though, his statue stands in major cities throughout Latin America, and Simón Bolívar is remembered as *El Libertador*, The Liberator.

Statue of Símon Bolívar in Paris

(continued from page 25)

Panama, the delegates signed treaties to cooperate in defending their countries. But once they returned home, most delegates failed to get their governments to ratify the treaties. Although Bolívar's federation was unsuccessful, it established an ideal of cooperation and collective security among the Americas.

HISTORICAL ROOTS OF THE OAS

The Congress of Panama was the first attempt to organize an inter-American union. In the following years, American states gathered for congresses, or meetings, as equal partners. When they wanted to establish similar laws and legal procedures or when they feared intervention by European nations, they held a congress and signed agreements.

While Latin American countries emphasized the importance of equality among member states, the United States had a different approach for organizing the hemisphere. The U.S. tradition started with President James Monroe in his annual message to Congress in 1823. He believed the newly independent colonial empires must remain free from intervention by European nations, with the United States as a kind of protector. President Monroe said any attempt to colonize or control these nations would show "an unfriendly disposition toward the United States."[9] His ideas became known as the Monroe Doctrine, and it was added to by later U.S. presidents, especially President Theodore Roosevelt. Instead of calling for a federation of equal nation-states, Roosevelt declared the Western Hemisphere to be the U.S. sphere of influence. This meant Roosevelt saw the United States as replacing Europe as a major trading partner and political power. As a result of this attitude, in the twentieth century Latin Americans often felt their sovereignty threatened by the powerful United States. Sometimes called the "Colossus of the North," the United States used military and financial might to interfere in the affairs of its southern neighbors, invading Latin American and the Caribbean states more than 20 times between 1899 and 1917.

The two opposing views, an alliance among equals and one where the United States dominates, have caused tension. Still, the countries of the Western Hemisphere have continued to want some sort of cooperative alliance.

Because U.S. business interests sought raw materials and markets in Latin America, in 1889 Secretary of State James G. Blaine organized the First International Conference of American States. He invited the American states to come to Washington, D.C. Blaine asked statesmen to discuss plans that "shall tend to preserve the peace and promote the prosperity of several American states. . . ."[10] The conference wanted to find ways to settle disputes among the countries and to improve business and communication in order to advance commercial relations and increase the markets for their products. Eighteen delegates from the American republics came to the conference. They discussed trade, commerce, tariffs, and customs laws, including rules and taxes on goods and raw materials that could be exported and imported among the states. They also considered ways to work together on political and cultural matters. They held more conferences and continued an alliance for inter-American cooperation. By 1910, it was known as the Pan American Union (PAU).

PAN AMERICAN UNION

The PAU served as an organization of American states until 1948. From its founding until World War II, several conferences took place. At these meetings, delegates discussed international law, copyrights, trademarks, loans by foreigners, commercial and business practices, and cultural understanding and social problems. Diplomats from Latin America and the United States signed treaties and conventions of agreement. To further their goals, these hemispheric conferences set up permanent inter-American agencies. For example, in 1902, the Pan American Sanitary Bureau, later called the Pan American Health Organization (PAHO), was established to improve health practices in the hemisphere. Other specialized agencies followed.

During most of these years, the U.S. government continued to follow the Monroe Doctrine in its dealings with its southern neighbors. But in the 1930s, U.S. President Franklin D. Roosevelt began the "Good Neighbor Policy." This new policy said the United States no longer wanted to send its military forces to fight or its battleships to threaten governments in order to keep its influence in Latin American. Instead, the United States tried humanitarian programs in education, health, and agriculture; cultural exchanges between citizens and students; and it rewarded local politicians who followed U.S. advice. In addition, the U.S. military trained countries' national-guard units. In 1933, the American states signed the Convention on the Rights and Duties of States. This declared the right of states to exist without intervention from outside states, the importance of peaceful settlement of conflicts, and nonacceptance of territorial conquest. These policies increased trust for the United States in the hemisphere. In 1938, American states established the Meeting of Consultation of Ministers of Foreign Affairs, which was to meet if any urgent matter needed attention, such as a conflict between member states. Thus, even before the outbreak of World War II, the American states had signed agreements concerned with peace and security.

THE OAS ESTABLISHED AT END OF WAR

At the end of the World War II, representatives gathered in Chapultepec, Mexico, in 1945 to discuss the future of inter-American relations. The foreign ministers of 20 American republics wanted to continue their solidarity, and they hoped the United States would continue the economic support it had given during the war. The foreign ministers pledged to deal with threats of intervention into any American state. They recommended a future treaty to specify what actions would be taken in the event of attack from outside the hemisphere

Consequently, in 1947, U.S. and Latin American representatives met in Rio de Janeiro, Brazil, and signed the Rio Treaty, promising to work together for protection but still remain sovereign states. The Rio Treaty pledged that an aggressive act against any American state would force an immediate meeting to decide what to do to keep peace. Because these countries had worked together in the past, it was easy for them to reach agreement. Even though they wanted to cooperate in solving some problems, they also wanted to remain independent states with their own governments, rules, and laws. The Rio Treaty was one piece of the cooperation they envisioned. These diplomats yearned to reorganize and strengthen past hemispheric agreements. Since the United States and its southern neighbors had been holding conferences, signing multilateral treaties, and setting up cooperative agencies for more than a hundred years, they wanted a new organization to formalize past agreements and treaties.

A year after signing the Rio Treaty, delegates gathered at a conference in Bogotá, Colombia. They passed 50 resolutions concerning the rights of women, democracy, human rights, colonies and territories, legal rights, and economic cooperation—all to start the inter-American system in a new direction. In addition, they signed the Pact of Bogotá, which pledged them to find peaceful settlement for conflicts among themselves. The Latin American countries and the United States, with the approval of the United Nations, then unanimously adopted the OAS charter. It created a permanent organization of the Western Hemisphere states that would perform many functions.

The U.S. government saw this new organization as a way to protect the region against the rise of international Communism. In the Cold War, differences between the United States and the Soviet Union meant each superpower wanted to protect its own sphere of influence. And since the Monroe Doctrine, the U.S. government had considered the Americas its region of influence. For many people in Latin America, though, the

OAS provided a means to give them an equal partnership with the United States. It was a way to protect themselves from U.S. military interventions. The United States had emerged from World War II as the wealthiest and most powerful nation in the global community. Latin Americans believed the OAS and U.S. aid would help build higher standards of living in the region.

THE OAS CHARTER

In addition to describing its goals and principles, the OAS charter explained the framework, or how the organization was to be set up and how it was to function. Today, the structure differs greatly from its earlier framework. The original charter accepted the idea of the Pan American Union, with conference meetings every few years. These conferences would be the highest decision-making body. The Meeting of Consultation of Ministers of Foreign Affairs (MCMFA), the conference of foreign ministers of member states, became a second major body. It would meet at least every five years. The third major body was the Council of the OAS (COAS). It was in constant session and supervised most activities and institutes established by the Pan American Union. The Inter-American Conferences, the MCMFA, and the COAS all had representatives from each country, and they determined political, legal, military, economic, and social policies. In reality, these bodies had little influence over hemispheric politics. Latin American states remained concerned with keeping their independence as governments, and the United States remained concerned with fighting Communism.

FAILURE OF POLITICAL PARTNERSHIP

The vision set forth by the OAS charter, though, reflected worthy principles and the highest ideals of the signers. But as an organization for solving political problems in the Americas, the OAS soon disappointed many Latin American leaders. These leaders had hoped to cooperate with the United States

Alberto Lleras Camargo was a journalist and politician before becoming director of the Pan American Union. Later he became the first secretary-general of the OAS, eventually leaving his position out of frustration. He later unseated Colombia's dictator and became president, where he ended 10 years of violent political conflicts and stabilized the economy.

as an equal partner. Instead of equality, many Latin American statesmen found the United States continued its unilateral, or single country, actions. Despite the calls for nonintervention into the affairs of other states, the United States continued to intervene with its armed forces into American countries. In addition, some Latin American nations fought their neighbors in border disputes. A few statesmen felt unhappy because other Latin American leaders failed to stand up to U.S. might and pressure. The first secretary-general of the OAS, Alberto

Lleras Camargo, was one leader who became discouraged with the organization.

Lleras, a Colombian, was elected secretary-general in 1948. Before this, he had been the director-general of the Pan American Union. In 1945, he had headed his country's delegation to the meetings in San Francisco, where the United Nations was established. Lleras was a practical man, and it was his desire to make the OAS run efficiently. After his election, he made annual reports to COAS and presented the problems as he saw them. These reports, he thought, would serve as a basis for solving hemisphere concerns. Instead, he found the diplomats more concerned with ceremonial and routine matters. He complained about governments' failure to come to the OAS to resolve disagreements, ignoring the potential force of the new organization. He believed the political problems of the hemisphere should be solved through the OAS, and both the secretary-general's office and the organization needed more authority.

Lleras's views were supported by some countries, which wished to strengthen COAS to take action. But some states were unwilling to grant the OAS more authority. Mexico, for one, feared the United States would interfere with its national sovereignty through the OAS. Lleras's frustration was so great that he finally resigned his post at a meeting in 1954 in Caracas, Venezuela. "The Organization," he said, "is neither good nor bad; it can be nothing else than what the governments which are members of the Organization want it to be."[11]

Cold War fears grew from the 1950s through the 1960s, as the United States remained focused on stopping Communism. The Latin Americans wanted sizable economic aid from the United States. Although the Colossus of the North had sent massive aid to rebuild Europe and Japan after World War II, it failed to develop an effective plan for Latin America. As a result, two different aims dominated the OAS agenda during these years. Although some economic aid programs were offered by the United States, these had little effect in dealing with Latin America's enormous economic and social problems. Most Latin Americans lived in the countryside and jungles, farming without electricity, running water, paved roads or adequate shelter. Some worked in foreign-owned industries such as mining, timber, or agriculture and received low wages.

In 1961, U.S. President John F. Kennedy announced the Alliance for Progress, to help the economic growth of Latin America and bring change to the region. The plan included programs to improve transportation, communication systems, and agriculture. Its misunderstanding of cultures and lack of lasting change as well as its methods for aid giving, though, brought little relief to the poor peoples of the hemisphere. Latin American leaders thought that if they could reform the OAS, it might better fit their needs. Chile's president Eduardo Frei Montalva was one of the leaders who called for change. He said, ". . . .the Organization of American States no longer has any real vitality. The moment is approaching for a decision whether to put it in line with a rapidly changing world and with the goals of the Alliance for Progress, or to let it become a coffin of out-moded ideas."[12]

Another crisis erupted for the OAS when 23,000 U.S. troops invaded the Dominican Republic in April 1965. President Lyndon B. Johnson completely bypassed the OAS and sent U.S. Marines to stop a government unfriendly to the United States from coming to power. In May, the U.S. representative asked for an inter-American military force to restore order in the Dominican Republic. Under pressure from the United States, the OAS voted 14 to 5 to support the U.S. resolution. A few countries sent troops to support the U.S. forces. Those countries opposed to such a mission felt the OAS had again bent to the will of the United States. To save the organization, a

Following the exile of leftist president Juan Bosch and the rise of pro-Bosch rebels who wanted to reinstate him as president, President Lyndon Johnson ordered U.S. troops be sent to the Dominican Republic in a maneuver called Operation Power Pack (April 1965–Sept. 1966). Initially, troops were there to evacuate foreign civilians, but eventually the troops and the OAS's inter-American military force were needed to restore order to the embattled country. With U.S. support, Joaquin Balaguer was elected president in 1966.

Special Inter-American Conference prepared a draft to reform the OAS and its charter.

FIRST PROTOCOL AND CHARTER AMENDMENTS

The first major charter improvements came in 1967 and were designed to give Latin Americans more power. The Protocol of Buenos Aires created the General Assembly as the major decision-making body, requiring it to hold meetings at least once a year. With more frequent contact, more problems could be dealt with together. Then, the old COAS became the Permanent Council and would meet throughout the year, developing working committees. Next, the amended charter set up a special agency, the Inter-American Commission on Human Rights (IACHR), to look into violations of human rights by member governments. Although the OAS charter opposed harmful acts against citizens, in the Dominican Republic, as in Guatemala and elsewhere, secret police still assassinated citizens who tried to reform their government. The organization needed an institute to deal with such crimes. With the establishment of the IACHR, the OAS placed greater emphasis on democratic and human rights. It might now be able to dampen U.S. backing of undemocratic governments. In addition, new amendments established three councils to focus on educational, scientific, economic, social, and cultural projects. Another major change in the charter was opening membership to newly independent colonies from the Caribbean, thus making the OAS a truly hemispheric organization.

This represented a real change in the nature of membership. Almost all the founding OAS countries were of Hispanic background, but the English-speaking Caribbean nations were culturally distinct. Their geography and small size created even more differences. As the delegates signed the amendment during the closing session of the conference, everyone was excited about a new spirit of international and regional cooperation. Many statesmen believed Latin America and the Caribbean could finally share decision-making power with the United States through the OAS. Addressing the assembly, Dr. Emilio Arenales, the Guatemalan foreign minister, said:

> The document we have just signed with such solemnity represents not merely a new state in an already long history of efforts by Americans to build systems making for constructive, harmonious international relationship, but also Latin America's redemption of its

own destiny. This, one might say has been the motto of our conference. The amendments to the Charter of the Organization on which we have agreed, make possible greater scope for us in the OAS by means of reorganization of its agencies, particularly by providing our annual obligation to attend the sovereign General Assembly; but they also reflect our increasing concern with the problems of cooperation and of development in the economic, social and cultural field.[13]

The charter changes supported a broader and more enduring organization, and seemed to encourage the OAS commitment to keeping peace and security in the hemisphere. The OAS intervened in a conflict between El Salvador and Honduras in 1969, and between Peru and Ecuador in the Condor Mountain Range in the 1980s, avoiding violent wars. It helped in the fall of the Somoza dictatorship in Nicaragua in 1979.

Despite hopes for more of a partnership with the Colossus of the North with the charter changes, Latin Americans found the United States continued to ignore the OAS charter. U.S. presidents intervened in Latin American countries when they disagreed with a government's policies. For example, President Richard Nixon aided a war against the democratically elected president of Chile, Salvador Allende. President Allende had put in place economic reforms that hurt U.S. business interests in Chile. With U.S. aid, a violent military coup eventually succeeded in 1973, and General Augusto Pinochet replaced Allende. Pinochet became a military dictator who ruled Chile with brutality for 16 years. A decade later, the United States completely ignored the sovereignty of Grenada, never consulted the OAS, and sent U.S. soldiers to invade the island. U.S. President Ronald Reagan said he was preventing a Communist takeover of the small Caribbean country. Because of these and other actions by the United States, many American leaders remained skeptical about the ability of the OAS to solve political disputes and to work cooperatively. Other Latin American diplomats thought they might achieve an organization with more equal power sharing with the United States if they could find the right reforms to the OAS charter.

As a result, more charter changes came at a meeting in Colombia in 1985. The General Assembly adopted changes granting the secretary-general more power. The amendments also gave the Permanent Council more authority to get countries together to work out disagreements. Other changes put into the OAS charter included the right of each country to determine how best to practice democracy as well as how to set up its economic system. Although more amendments passed in later years, the current structure of the OAS had been established.

How the
OAS Works

IN JULY 2007, THE OAS OFFERED TO SET UP AN INTERNATIONAL commission in Colombia to help with the return of 11 bodies of Colombian lawmakers killed in captivity. The lawmakers had been kidnapped from a government building in the city of Cali by the Revolutionary Armed Forces of Colombia (FARC). The government claimed the rebels killed the lawmakers, but FARC said they got caught in a crossfire. Whatever the cause of death, the relatives anxiously awaited the return of the bodies. In one of its many roles, the OAS called upon the authorities to take the steps necessary for the return of the bodies, saying, "The OAS stands ready to receive the bodies at an agreed location."[14]

The OAS performs wide-ranging missions, both large and small, through its many institutions. As its charter changed,

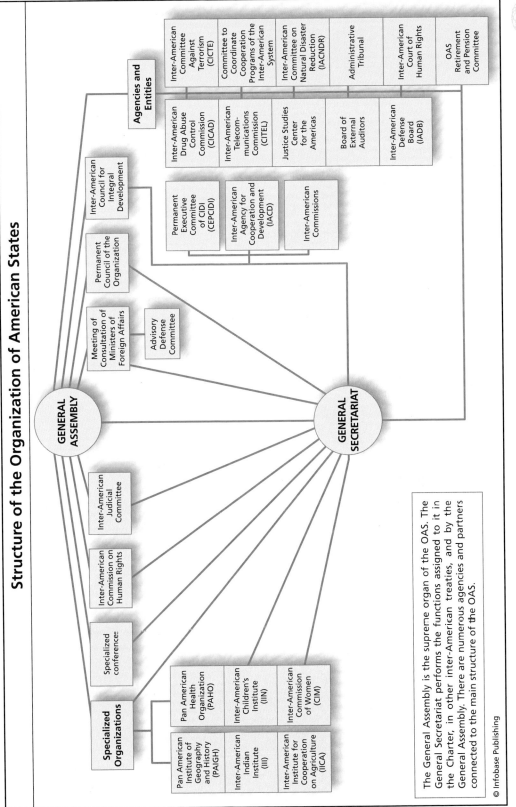

Structure of the Organization of American States

Agencies and Entities

- Inter-American Committee Against Terrorism (CICTE)
- Committee to Coordinate Cooperation Programs of the Inter-American System
- Inter-American Committee on Natural Disaster Reduction (IACNDR)
- Administrative Tribunal
- Inter-American Court of Human Rights
- OAS Retirement and Pension Committee
- Inter-American Drug Abuse Control Commission (CICAD)
- Inter-American Telecommunications Commission (CITEL)
- Justice Studies Center for the Americas
- Board of External Auditors
- Inter-American Defense Board (IADB)

GENERAL ASSEMBLY

GENERAL SECRETARIAT

Inter-American Council for Integral Development

- Permanent Executive Committee of CIDI (CEPCIDI)
- Inter-American Agency for Cooperation and Development (IACD)
- Inter-American Commissions

Permanent Council of the Organization

Meeting of Consultation of Ministers of Foreign Affairs
- Advisory Defense Committee

Inter-American Judicial Committee

Inter-American Commission on Human Rights

Specialized conferences

Specialized Organizations

- Pan American Health Organization (PAHO)
- Inter-American Children's Institute (IIN)
- Inter-American Commission of Women (CIM)
- Pan American Institute of Geography and History (PAIGH)
- Inter-American Indian Institute (III)
- Inter-American Institute for Cooperation on Agriculture (IICA)

The General Assembly is the supreme organ of the OAS. The General Secretariat performs the functions assigned to it in the Charter, in other inter-American treaties, and by the General Assembly. There are numerous agencies and partners connected to the main structure of the OAS.

© Infobase Publishing

both its activities and structure altered. Today the major bodies include the General Assembly and the General Secretariat, with the support from the Permanent Council, Inter-American Council for Integral Development, and the Meeting of the Council of Ministers of Foreign Affairs.

GENERAL ASSEMBLY

The General Assembly is a democratic body that meets once a year. Each member state gets one vote, but the head of any delegation may give his or her voting power to another member of the group. The national delegations include advisors who know the needs and desires of their governments. In addition to these voting members, representatives of the specialized organizations or committees and permanent observers of the OAS participate in General Assembly meetings. The secretary-general of the United Nations and representatives of other international agencies can also attend and give speeches or provide information.

In past years, some delegations of American states attending the General Assembly had represented undemocratic governments. During the brutal military regimes of 1960s–1990s in countries such as Nicaragua, Chile, and Argentina, the OAS took little action to bar their delegations from attending meetings. As the Cold War ended, though, many diplomats wanted to turn their attention to increasing democratic governments.

As a result, in 1991, a real breakthrough regarding military regimes took place when the General Assembly passed Resolution 1080. This resolution required an emergency meeting should the military overthrow the elected government in any member state. Resolution 1080 set a new direction for the principle of nonintervention, indicating the OAS was now willing to oppose the undemocratic behavior of leaders of member states. In 1992, the General Assembly again amended the charter to permit further actions to suspend governments that came to power illegally. The General Assembly could direct

According to human rights groups, between 11,000 and 30,000 people were killed or "disappeared" during the so-called Dirty War in Argentina. General Jorge Rafael Videla and members of the *junta* (committee) that overthrew President Isabel Peron claimed that "different" methods were needed to maintain order against guerrilla activity. Mainly the general population, students, trade unionists, and political opposition were subject to abductions, torture, "death flights" (people pushed out of planes over the Atlantic Ocean), and executions.

the secretary-general to call the Permanent Council to meet and consider ways to keep the country under democratic rule. These established a major step toward maintaining democratic governments in Latin America and the Caribbean.

Although the General Assembly continues to stress the importance of democratic governments, its diplomats shape policy on other challenges as well. The delegations have dealt with corruption in government. The General Assembly also discusses the environment, how to protect it, and how best to use the natural resources of the Americas. In recent years, the problem of illegal drugs has become enormous, and it has received much attention in the General Assembly. The illegal drug trade thrives in South America and Mexico because the geography of much of the region provides a good environ- ment for growing plants that can be used for these drugs. With people living in poverty, illegal plants provide income, and government officials can be easily bribed. In addition, many Native American cultures used mind-altering drugs in religious ceremonies or in daily life. With a ready market in the United States, these conditions combine to make it dif- ficult to control the illegal drug trade. Increasing concerns of terrorism have also required the diplomats' consideration in recent years. With its yearly meetings, the General Assembly sets the policies to deal with major concerns, but it is the secretary-general's office that undertakes much of the work of solving these problems.

GENERAL SECRETARIAT

The Office of General Secretariat coordinates most of the activities and programs. This office is headed by the secretary- general and the assistant secretary-general. They are elected for five-year terms and can be reelected once. Since the found- ing of the OAS, the candidate suggested by the United States to be secretary-general was always elected to the office. In 2005, though, that situation changed.

On October 8, 2004, shortly after the yearly meeting of the General Assembly, Secretary-General Miguel Ángel Rodríguez announced his resignation from the office. As a former presi- dent of Costa Rica, he faced charges of receiving bribes while in office. His attention was required at home.

Assistant Secretary-General Luigi R. Einaudi of the United States took over, but several diplomats requested a special session of the General Assembly to elect a new secretary-general. The wait for the next yearly meeting in June was too long, so names for successors circulated. The U.S. State Department announced it wanted the past president of El Salvador, Francisco Flores. Mexican President Vicente Fox nominated Luis Ernesto Derbez, Mexico's foreign minister to the post. A few days later, the Chilean government declared its candidate, Interior Minister José Miguel Insulza. A meeting was set for April, and various countries decided which candidate they would support. Just three days before the meeting, with almost no support, Flores withdrew his name. On April 11, 2005, the representatives gathered to choose their leader from the two remaining candidates. Although the delegates voted five times, each round ended in a 17 to 17 tie. Never in the history of the OAS had this happened. It was decided that the election would be rescheduled for May 2.

In the meantime, negotiations among diplomats went on for both candidates. In late April, it was announced that Derbez of Mexico was withdrawing. Thus, at the OAS meeting on May 2, 2005, Insulza was elected to the office. He became the new secretary-general of the OAS, and he made history as the first candidate to win who had not been chosen by the United States.

In his acceptance speech, Secretary-General Insulza said there were a few basic challenges in the hemisphere. He spoke of the need for fresh approaches, diversity, human rights, and security. The problems of violence and drug trafficking needed more attention. He said there must be continued and lasting economic growth, but the benefits of that growth must be shared with more people. Almost immediately, Insulza added new departments to help his office deal with these issues.

THE PERMANENT COUNCIL

Although the Permanent Council reports directly to the General Assembly, it works closely with the secretary-general. The Permanent Council is based in Washington, D.C., with one ambassador from each member state, and meets at least every two

JOSÉ MIGUEL INSULZA SALINAS, THE PANZER

On a September day in 1973, the streets of Santiago, Chile, filled with tanks and armed forces. Shots echoed through the streets, as bullets lodged into the government building. The Chilean military led by General Augusto Pinochet was overthrowing the democratically elected government of Salvador Allende. People stayed locked in their homes, fearing the violent military coup. José Miguel Insulza Salinas was one government official who escaped. He made it to Italy, but many of his friends, including Allende, died or disappeared as the brutal military dictatorship of Pinochet took over Chile.

Insulza was born in Santiago in 1943 and went to high school at Colegio de St. George. There he formed a friendship with Allende. Insulza went on to law school and to the University of Michigan. Returning home, he began life as a college professor and joined the socialist Popular Union Party. In 1970, his old schoolmate Allende became president, and Insulza worked in the new government, bringing what was called the Chilean Road to Socialism, until he was forced into exile. He lived abroad until democracy returned. Then, Insulza served under each of the democratically presidents until May 2005.

Early in his political career, he earned the nickname "Panzer"— for a German tank that took an attack with little damage. One attack happened when Insulza went to London to try to return weeks. Throughout the year, it carries on continuing programs and tries to keep good relationships among the member countries, the United Nations, and other international bodies.

The Permanent Council can be called upon to act to preserve democracies. If the Permanent Council meets to examine

José Miguel Insulza, secretary-general of the OAS

Pinochet to Chile. The ex-dictator had traveled to England and been put under arrest to stand trial for his human rights violations. Insulza argued for Pinochet's return to Chile, saying the Chilean courts should try Pinochet, not Spanish or English courts. In 2005, the Chilean government nominated Insulza for secretary-general of the OAS. This, too, became a battle. The Panzer, though, survived and became the secretary-general.

the undemocratic behavior of a member, it has 10 days to call a special session of the General Assembly or a Meeting of the Consultation of the Ministers of Foreign Affairs. MCMFA is made up of the foreign affairs advisors of member countries. It is called to discuss urgent problems. The Permanent Council must recommend peaceful procedures, such as a trade embargo with the problem state. The OAS may also vote to suspend the offending country's membership in the organization. This means if any member state loses its democratic government, the country could be excluded from OAS activities. This was a second major step toward keeping the hemisphere democratic.

In recent years, the OAS has acted when problems arose in Haiti, Peru, Paraguay, and Guatemala. In Peru, for example, on April 5, 1992, President Alberto Fujimori dissolved the Peruvian Congress when it began to investigate killings done by members of his military intelligence. He acted outside the law by dismissing the elected representatives of the people. The OAS Permanent Council immediately called for the return of "democratic institutions and respect for human rights under the rule of law."[15] The MCMFA met seven days later and demanded a return to democracy in Peru. They also directed the secretary-general, then Cesar Gavaria of Colombia, to lead a group of foreign ministers to Peru to work with the government and representatives of citizens to restore legal practices. A month later, President Fujimori agreed to call for elections for a new congress. Although more problems arose with the Fujimori government eight years later, the OAS efforts were successful in restoring democracy for a few years before it had to act again. With its actions against Peru and other member states, the OAS finally found some success in dealing with the political problem of undemocratic governments.

OTHER AGENCIES AND BODIES
Several other organizations connect in some way with the General Assembly and the General Secretariat, and new agen-

cies, programs, and projects arise as needed. Recently, the OAS has examined terrorism and passed many measures that deal with illegal arms and ammunition. An agency called the Inter-American Committee Against Terrorism (CICTE) allows member states to work together to control borders and share information about possible terrorists. Through CICTE, the OAS developed the world's first listing of antipersonnel land mines, and the United Nations followed with a global register.

Because of the rise of illegal drug trafficking, the OAS set up a commission that encourages members to strengthen antidrug laws and educate citizens on prevention. It spreads information from member states to slow the trafficking of illegal narcotics and money laundering. One project tries to help farmers find other crops to make money besides poppy, coca, and marijuana plants.

Another commission assists countries with their information technology and helps citizens learn to use computers and other new devices. Advancement in technology is essential for Latin American and Caribbean countries to take part in the global community and to increase their economic growth. Through various programs citizens are being trained and countries' systems are being updated to participate in the global technological revolution.

The list of OAS agencies and partners goes on and on. Today, the OAS institutions help solve the hemisphere's problems with its many agencies and institutions.

A NEW AGREEMENT: THE INTER-AMERICAN DEMOCRATIC CHARTER

Although the original OAS charter said that a true union of the American states was based on democratic institutions, it did little to support democracy. The charter upheld the rights of each country as a sovereign state to act on its own. With Resolution 1080 and the charter amendments in 1992, the OAS declared it would take action. No longer would the OAS tolerate military dictators who seized power. Step by step, the OAS was pushing its members to act inside the rules of international law and political constitutions.

Some Latin American delegates felt more was needed to support democracy in the hemisphere. Others consented, and work began on a new agreement for the OAS. At a special meeting in Lima, Peru, in 2001, the General Assembly adopted the Inter-American Democratic Charter. The OAS accepted new definitions of democratic governments. The charter stated:

> The people of the Americas have a right to democracy and their governments have an obligation to promote and defend it. The essential elements of representative democracy include..., respect for human rights and fundamental freedoms..., the holding of periodic, free, and fair elections based on secret balloting and universal suffrage [voting].... Transparency [openness] in government activities..., [and] respect for social rights and freedom of expression and of the press are essential components of the exercise of democracy. The promotion and strengthening of democracy requires the full and effective exercise of workers' rights..., as recognized in the International Labour Organization (ILO).... Poverty, illiteracy, and low levels of human development are factors that adversely affect the consolidation of democracy.[16]

The Inter-American Democratic Charter defined what governments must do to provide democracy. Yet, it fell short by failing to forbid some practices usually associated with nondemocratic governments. For example, closing down newspapers that disagreed with government policies or stopping opposition political parties—all antidemocratic measures— were not specifically banned. Some states wanted to see these rules added, but others were unwilling to add these provisions. The charter had to be a compromise so that all the countries would sign it. The Colombian ambassador to the OAS and the debate leader, Humberto de la Calle, believed the charter brought as much reform as OAS members would accept. He said, "We have updated old agreements, and we have gone as far as the OAS rules allow us to go."[17]

Although methods for carrying out democracy in the hemisphere remain incomplete, the Inter-American Democratic Charter represented another step on the road toward supporting it. It is now a major document and allows the OAS to identify some undemocratic practices of repressive governments.

WORKING AGAINST CORRUPTION IN MEMBER STATES

Even with the Inter-American Democratic Charter, corruption remains a problem for democratic governments. For years, corrupt government officials have used their offices to improve their own wealth. They often robbed treasuries, gave relatives or friends government contracts, took bribes, passed legislation that enriched them or their friends, or lived lavish lifestyles while ordinary citizens struggled with daily life. As a result, citizens have little faith in their public officials. In 2005, polling firm Latinobarometro reported 69 percent of Latin Americans felt unhappy with their governments. A full 70 percent believed that there was a great deal of corruption in their governments from the national to the local level. In addition, people thought little was being done to stop it. The patterns of power often follow the colonial traditions of greed and corruption. Even leaders who were elected to fight crime and fraud in their countries find it hard to end bribery in government. Mexican President Vicente Fox, for example, came to office in 2000 and ran on a platform to stop government corruption. In 2005, though, he was forced to send the army

In 2005, hundreds of police officers and soldiers conducted a raid to regain control of maximum-security prison La Palma, in Mexico. Home to some of the most notorious drug traffickers in the country, cartel leaders continued to run operations from their cells. Prison employees and top officials are said to have been involved in the corruption, allowing prisoners special privileges including plasma TVs and cell phones, and overlooking the murders of people inside and outside the prison.

into La Palma prison from which drug lords had been operating. These drug lords had bribed the guards and wardens and used the prison as headquarters for their criminal operation. Such activities are common, and often those elected by the people are part of the problem. Even former OAS ministers and diplomats have been charged with corruption in their home countries. Recent scandals in the U.S. Congress show that fraud and bribery are not limited to Latin America and the Caribbean.

Early in his term, Secretary-General José Miguel Insulza stated that maintaining democracy under the Democratic Charter required fighting corruption in government. At a meeting of anticorruption experts he said:

> Governments have to continually be more efficient in tackling and resolving people's problems, but at the same time they have to be more transparent in formulating and implementing their public policies and practices. They need to vigorously punish corruption committed by public officials as well as by the private interests that corrupt them.[18]

Often in the past, dishonest officials have robbed their country of monies and assets that belong to the state. Then, they have gone to live in other countries such as the United States, Europe, or other Latin American states. One example is Anastasio Somoza of Nicaragua, who in 1979 fled first to the United States and then settled in Paraguay. Beginning in the 1930s, his family started amassing huge wealth while heading the Nicaraguan government. Since 2004, the members of the OAS have agreed to deny such crooked officials safe places to live. They have also agreed to strengthen laws that allow the illegally taken funds and assets to be returned to the public treasuries. But passing resolutions and enforcing them require different actions, and the OAS has few means of making members comply if they refuse.

Although a major interest of the OAS is the continuance of democracy, poverty remains a huge unsolved problem. Even today, more than half of all the people in Latin America and the Caribbean live without adequate jobs, shelter, or opportunities to improve their lives. This terrible situation has changed little since the founding of the OAS. In recent years, the OAS has emphasized the importance of decreasing poverty as a way to keep democracy strong. The Protocol of Managua in 1993 created the Inter-American Council for Integral Development (CIDI) to work toward solutions. So far, though, there has been little lasting change in most of the poor developing countries.

Poverty:
A Problem
for the OAS

TODAY, MANY OF THE WORLD'S POOREST PEOPLE LIVE IN LATIN America and the Caribbean. In the decade of the 1990s, there was a slight decrease in extreme poverty in Latin America, but hundreds of thousands of people still face hunger and lack sufficient shelter. The distance between "the haves" and "the have-nots" remains large. Those living in poverty are frequently sick but are too poor to get medical help. Because impoverished families need money to live, their children have to help earn a living and usually do not attend school or learn to read.

POVERTY IN LATIN AMERICA
AND THE CARIBBEAN
In the countryside, the rich have traditionally owned the land. Since colonial times, poor laborers have lived and worked on

Brazil has some of the poorest populations in South America, with about 20 million rural poor people. The children pictured live in the Gloria slum above the Amazon River in Manaus, Brazil, about a mile from huge corporations like Nokia, Siemens, Harley-Davidson, and Honda.

huge plantations owned by the wealthy or, more recently, huge corporations. People known as tenant farmers or sharecroppers plant, weed, and harvest the crops. But because they lack ownership of the land, they collect only half or less of what they produce. Even recent programs for land reform, such as giving land to these tenant farmers, have often failed. Without money to buy seeds and with no way to store or get crops to market, poor farmers still cannot make a decent living. Even for people who have left the countryside and migrated to the cities to look for work, deep poverty continues. Many of these migrants end up living in the slums and squatter cities on the outskirts of towns and cities. They are desperate to get jobs and make a living, but they lack the skills or there are no jobs available. Many people labor in the informal sector, meaning they find whatever they can do to earn money. This might be anything from collecting scrap metal for a few dollars to selling ears of corn on the street. Extremely poor people in the hemisphere live from one day to the next with little hope of improving their situation.

There is much debate as to how best to improve the economic growth of the developing countries while advancing the economic well-being of all levels of society. So far programs and projects in Latin America and the Caribbean have failed to close the gap in the standard of living between the north—the United States and Canada—and the rest of the hemisphere. Latin America and the Caribbean started far below their northern neighbors, but too many people have been left behind as the world modernized. Although U.S. corporations and a few elites in some countries prospered, few projects brought sustained or long-term help for the majority of peoples of the Americas. With most of the wealth, income, and land in the hands of a few, it is difficult for the poor to take part in their economic system.

In the past, too, development projects neglected to involve local agencies and organizations in their planning and

activities. Instead, they used outside experts to solve problems. At times, these experts failed to understand or take into
account the culture or traditions of the local people. Often the
projects lacked sustainable or lasting results. Although many
Latin Americans hoped from the beginning that the OAS could
deal with economic problems and growth, it has proved unsuccessful in reducing either inequality or poverty. As a result,
many of the countries began to look for help for their problem
in different alliances.

REGGAE: FROM SHANTYTOWN TO POP CULTURE

On the Caribbean island of Jamaica, from the streets of a Kingston
slum, the global pop sounds of reggae were born. Bob Marley, a
poor teenager working in a welding shop, loved music and used
his spare time to learn guitar and play in bands. Marley and his
friends knew traditional Jamaican and African music and beats;
it was part of their street culture. On the radio, they heard Ray
Charles, Fats Domino, and the sounds of rhythm and blues coming from the United States. Marley and his friends formed a band
called the "Wailing Wailins" and got the opportunity to record
some of their music.

The new sound they played came from the music they had
heard. But their songs had a new rhythm, and the words often
came from their life experiences living in poverty, facing racial discrimination, and their beliefs as Rastafarians, a religion of Jamaica.
The music eventually became known as reggae or root reggae.
The lyrics include criticism of colonial governments, colonial education systems, imperialism, and other political systems that keep

AMERICAN STATES AND SUBREGIONAL AGREEMENTS

Latin Americans and peoples from the Caribbean want political, economic, and cultural equality as they seek a place in the global community. As a result, many formed subregional or local alliances to work as one market because they wanted to improve their economic growth and maintain their independence. By forming a common market, they could gain economic influence and overcome the problems faced by small countries conducting

people poor. The words of reggae songs promote black pride and nationalism. They are antiracist, anticapitalist, and antimaterialist, and they urge people to action against injustice. In "Get Up, Stand Up!" Marley wrote: "So now we see the light/We gonna stand up for our right." In his "Redemption Songs" he sang: "Emancipate yourselves from mental slavery/None but yourself can free your mind." Marley's singing and style spread reggae from Jamaica to the world. As a guitarist, he played his songs all over the United States, Europe, and other lands. Some of Marley's biggest hits have been recorded many times and by many people. In "I Shot the Sheriff," Marley writes about social justice. In "One Love/One People," he calls for global unity.

In Jamaica, dreadlocks became popular as black racial pride increased with a new popular culture. Unfortunately, Marley got cancer, and the disease shortened his life. Still, the sounds and culture of reggae arose from Marley and other poor blacks living on a poor Caribbean island. And they created a new style of music and pop culture.

business and trade with bigger states. The Caribbean region, for example, started a common market, CARICOM, to work toward an integrated or single economic system.

For several years, the Caribbean countries worked to create a free trade zone. They signed various agreements to remove tariffs, or taxes, on goods traded among their island states. In 1973, they signed the Treaty of Chaguaramas establishing CARICOM. With this subregional common market, the countries attempted to have the same tariff for outside goods coming in and to allow the free movement of workers and businesses from one island to another. They wanted to provide more jobs and wider employment opportunities for their citizens. During the 1990s, as globalization—the global marketplace—grew, the Caribbean states feared they might have even less economic and political clout. Consequently, the Caribbean region sought broader economic and political integration. CARICOM built links with countries in Central and South America, and with Mexico and Cuba. Although some of its products, such as bananas, compete in the global marketplace, CARICOM worked to expand and coordinate trade, economic opportunities, and political security. CARICOM has membership in other subregional groups, and this has helped increase its integration into South America. It strengthened cooperation in trade, transportation methods, and energy policies. These arrangements offered CARICOM ways to promote its regional interests in the global community. Caribbean countries also have bilateral agreements with the United States, which has allowed them free trade on some of their products.

South American countries also made attempts to integrate their economic systems. Brazil, Argentina, Paraguay, and Uruguay wanted to start a customs union to get rid of different rules, or nontariff barriers, and tariffs on goods and even services, such as accounting and insurance. For many years, they negotiated to eliminate tariffs and nontariff barriers against goods and services coming into their countries. They wanted a free exchange of goods and services among themselves. From earlier agreements and subregional groups, the Common Market of the South (MERCOSUR) emerged after the signing of the Treaty of Asunción in 1995. Today, in addition to the original members, its associate members include Venezuela, Bolivia, Colombia, Peru, Chile, and a CARICOM representative. MERCOSUR negotiates with other countries, groups of countries (such as the European Union), and even international organizations. MERCOSUR members cooperate on education, energy, the environment, agriculture, and political policies.

Another subregional group that operates in the area is the Rio Group. When Latin American states found their needs not being met by the U.S.-manipulated OAS, they formed an alternative alliance. The Rio Group, with 19 South and Central American countries and CARICOM, meets annually to work cooperatively to increase their political, economic, social, scientific, and technological cooperation. These countries, though, continue to take part in the OAS.

In 1992, the United States, Canada, and Mexico signed the North American Free Trade Association (NAFTA), agreeing to create a free trade area among the three countries. Some tariffs and nontariff barriers were immediately dropped, such as those on computers, cars, and most agricultural crops. Other products, like wood, were to be added over time. Within two years, because of concerns for the environment and for the rights and conditions of workers, new agreements were added to NAFTA. Mexico had fewer environmental laws and fewer health and safety rules for its workers. Without equal health, safety, and environmental protection, it would be cheaper to make certain products. This would give Mexico an advantage over its northern partners. Unlike a customs union, all three countries were allowed to sign different trade treaties with other countries. Mexico, for example, has several free trade arrangements with trading partners in the Caribbean and Latin America.

There has been much disagreement about the benefits and harm of NAFTA. Some workers in the United States have lost jobs to lower-paid workers in Mexico in the same industries. The hourly wage for production workers in Mexico has gone down, and many poor Mexican farmers have lost their land. They are unable to compete with U.S. farmers who receive government subsidies, or money, for growing their products. Independent farmers in all three countries have lost farmland to giant agricultural businesses. With more food available for export, hunger increased among the poor. The Canadian government has complained that the United States has failed to allow some of its products to enter the country. Nonetheless, the amount of trade between the partners has increased, and many products have become cheaper to buy. Most economists agree that free trade can be beneficial to countries. Governments, though, must make certain that the poorest citizens have ways to get resources, good employment opportunities, and freedom from hunger and want. Without these assurances, free trade hurts the poor.

SUMMIT OF THE AMERICAS

When the OAS wanted help solving major problems in Latin America and the Caribbean, it urged U.S. presidents to hold a summit meeting of the American states. In the 1950s and 1960s, both U.S. presidents Dwight D. Eisenhower and Lyndon B. Johnson called an American summit, inviting all the heads-of-state. In 1994, after almost 30 years, U.S. President Bill Clinton decided to hold another summit. The U.S. Department of State sent invitations to the heads-of-state of the Western Hemispheric countries to come and discuss the region's most pressing concerns. Thirty-three heads-of-state met in Miami, Florida. Diplomats had been working for months to draw up future plans for the hemisphere. The occasion represented many firsts in summit history. It was the first time all the leaders came from democratically elected governments. It was the first time such a summit included Canada and the Caribbean states. In addition, it was the first time all the heads-of-state were seated around one table.

President Clinton gave the opening remarks at a reception in the Biltmore Hotel Country Club. Looking around a room filled with America's leaders, the U.S. Congress, business leaders, and representatives of nongovernmental organizations, President Clinton gave a hearty welcome to all. "The end of the cold war," he began, "has given all of us a great opportunity to build bridges where, for 50 years, only barriers stood." He said:

> This week we have come together to build a better world and a better future for our children. Students of the Americas will recognize this as an old dream. In the 1820s, at the dawn of freedom for the new Latin American republics, Simón Bolívar dreamed the Americas could be the greatest region on Earth, . . . Now, some 170 years later Bolívar's dream for the Americas is becoming a reality. Our goals for the summit are clear: We want to extend free trade from Alaska to Argentina, we want to strengthen our democracies, and we want to improve the quality of life for all our people. [19]

The First Summit of the Americas addressed problems in the hemisphere and discussed strengthening democracy and decreasing poverty. It formed a partnership with the OAS. The leaders attending the First Summit agreed with President Clinton that a Free Trade Area of the Americas (FTAA) might rid the hemisphere of extreme poverty. The Second Summit—in Santiago, Chile, in 1998—called for all countries to agree to the FTAA by 2005. Within three years, though, the goal for the FTAA became quite controversial.

When the Third Summit of the Americas was held in Quebec City, Canada, in 2001, more than 20,000 protesters marched through the streets of the city. They opposed the provisions of the trade treaty. From across the Americas,

In April 2001, 34 heads of state from the Americas met to discuss ways to lower trade barriers throughout the Americas and the Caribbean. Intended to provide intensive security measures, a nine-foot-high fence of concrete and wire was constructed around the meeting site to restrict the movement of antiglobalization protestors. The summit attracted 20,000 people from all over the Americas, with some protestors clashing violently with police.

environmental groups such as Greenpeace, human rights groups such as Americas Watch, trade union workers such as those from the International Labor Organization, and non-governmental organizations came to Canada. They believed the treaty would bring problems rather than assistance to the peoples of the Americas. The treaty, they said, gave benefits to large nations over small, to U.S. corporations over Latin American and Caribbean interests, and it failed to protect the environment and workers in poor developing countries. Most of the demonstrators were peaceful, but others turned violent.

The police erected fences around the meeting hall and kept the protesters out. Inside, the leaders worked toward completion of the FTAA treaty. In 2004, at a special summit in Monterrey, Mexico, stressing sustainable development (lasting growth), all was quiet. Just one year later, though, there were more protests against the FTAA.

At the seaside resort of Mar del Plata, in Argentina, the Fourth Summit of the Americas was held while demonstrators crowded the town. Security was tight, and three chain-link fences kept back the huge crowds. Many protesters held signs and chanted against U.S. President George W. Bush, who was pushing the FTAA treaty. Inside the summit, President Néstor Kirchner of Argentina blamed the U.S.-backed economic policies for his country's financial crisis. The presidents of Brazil, Uruguay, Venezuela, and Paraguay said they, too, opposed what they considered U.S. dominance of their economic systems through the FTAA. These countries were afraid local businesses would lose out to more powerful U.S. firms, and their citizens would fail to gain benefits. All five presidents refused to sign the FTAA treaty. The theme of the Mar del Plata summit was "Creating Jobs to Fight Poverty and Strengthen Democratic Governance." This was a theme everyone agreed on, and all the leaders signed a declaration and an action plan to create jobs and strengthen democracy. The two goals of eliminating poverty and supporting democracy were now tied together.

NEW ECONOMIC AGENCIES FOR THE OAS

The OAS has remained concerned about the problems of the poor, and in 1993, the General Assembly voted to establish the Inter-American Council for Integral Development (CIDI). It would be a major body to work for economic improvement for each level of the society. Member states can apply for grants to create their own projects, which will develop and educate their citizens or help increase employment, build needed services, or integrate the economy. With the charter amendment creating CIDI, the OAS pledged to bring equal opportunity so more people could participate fully in their own development and improvement.

The policies used to fight poverty come from the General Assembly, the Permanent Council, and the Summit of the Americas. The OAS serves two major roles in promoting economic development. It raises monies to support projects, and it encourages cooperation among countries for solving economic problems. Besides the CIDI, the OAS has several agencies that deal with development.

Secretary-General Insulza established the Executive Secretariat for Integral Development (SEDI) to work with projects involving education, culture, science and technology, labor, sustainable development, the environment, tourism, and trade. It wants to aid member states by training teachers and citizens, creating employment opportunities, and strengthening local agencies and democratic institutions. A major goal is to allow the governments' agencies to use information technologies to share experiences. One project funded through SEDI involved the managers and hotel owners of small hotels in Central America. Hundreds of people took part in courses, which trained them in giving quality service, using computer technologies, and managing hotels. Some courses took place in central locations, but others were video and TV programs.

Only time will tell if these new approaches and institutions will eventually end hunger and malnutrition, raise living standards, reduce poverty in the hemisphere, and bring benefits to lower levels of society. The OAS has supported a growing number of programs dealing with economic development and poverty, so far with little success. In addition, it has six specialized organizations that work on practical problems such as health or children's rights. Because poverty remains a major problem, all six of these organizations deal with it in some way.

Specialized Organizations of the OAS

"THE WAR AGAINST POLIO IS NEARLY OVER. VICTORY HAS BEEN achieved in the Western Hemisphere with eradication of the disease from the Americas."[20] This was announced by three doctors from the Pan American Health Organization (PAHO). It was a great day in 1997 for PAHO, the World Health Organization (WHO), Rotary International, UNICEF (the UN Children's Fund), and the U.S. Centers for Disease Control (CDC). As often happens, an OAS agency partnered with other organizations to bring success.

PAHO was the first permanent inter-American bureau established by the Pan American Union (PAU). It was named the Pan American Sanitary Bureau, later called PAHO, but five other organizations followed. When the OAS began, these six organizations became its partners. They operate independently and have their own staff of experts. They set their own goals, although they take suggestions from the OAS.

PAHO

The Pan American Health Organization is the oldest health organization in the global community. Its original goals were to improve health and sanitation standards. Although its central office was located in Washington, D.C., in 1923 it began to set up sites across the Americas. Its central mission was to teach people health standards and to stop the spread of disease. According to historian O. Carlos Stoetzer, it worked in the Americas for many years "to fight disease, prolong life, and encourage the physical and mental improvement of their peoples."[21]

After more than 40 years in operation, though, the health organization faced a crisis. In 1946, WHO decided unilaterally to have PAHO become its agency in the Western Hemisphere. Latin American administrators and doctors working in PAHO took offense at the failure to be consulted. They represented the first independent health organization, and they refused to be swallowed up by the world organization. It took a year before the two groups agreed PAHO could act as an arm of WHO and still remain self-governing. Thus, it operates with WHO but concentrates on the health problems of the Americas.

What PAHO Does

Both the charter of the OAS and the Inter-American Declaration of Human Rights state health care is a right of citizens. PAHO works with governments to provide health coverage for their people. Today, it has 27 country offices and nine scientific research centers. PAHO partners with each country's office of health and trains health-care workers. One of its most important missions is to help countries share information and health practices. In fighting disease and promoting health, it especially tries to assist mothers, children, the elderly, the poor, workers, displaced persons, and refugees. One major goal is to reduce the number of infants who die before they reach the age of five. It provides on-the-ground coverage for disasters and disease outbreaks. Although PAHO works on all health issues, in the 1950s it began campaigns to fight malaria, smallpox, yellow fever, leprosy, and other contagious diseases. These diseases are often the result of jungle climates with infection-bearing insects or unsanitary conditions and close contact with many people. Medicine can stop these sicknesses and save lives. As a result, PAHO doctors got together and started to work on vaccinating all the children in the hemisphere against preventable diseases.

PAHO Wipes Out Smallpox and Polio

PAHO started with smallpox, a disease that causes pimples or pockmarks and often leaves big scars. Through a special fund, it bought drugs and began a process of immunization. By 1980, it had eliminated smallpox from the Americas. The next attempt was to get rid of polio, a disease that attacks muscles and cripples or even kills its victims. Dr. Ciro de Quadros, a Brazilian epidemiologist (a doctor who works on diseases that spread easily), developed a plan for giving oral vaccines invented by Dr. Jonas Salk. Oral treatments can be easily carried by health-care workers to rural villages and into the jungles and countryside. It is simpler to give medicine by mouth than by an injection. Dr. Quadros wanted to form country-wide campaigns and reach all children up to age six. PAHO workers in each country chose a week to cover the entire region, vaccinating children throughout the country. These were called National Immunization Days, and each country in Latin America and the Caribbean held them. They were publicized through TV, radio, posters, schools, and word of mouth. Once children got their dose, they were marked with indelible ink, or as in Brazil, a stamp called Little Drop to show they had received their medicine.

These campaigns became so important to people that, despite civil wars in Peru and El Salvador, fighting stopped so

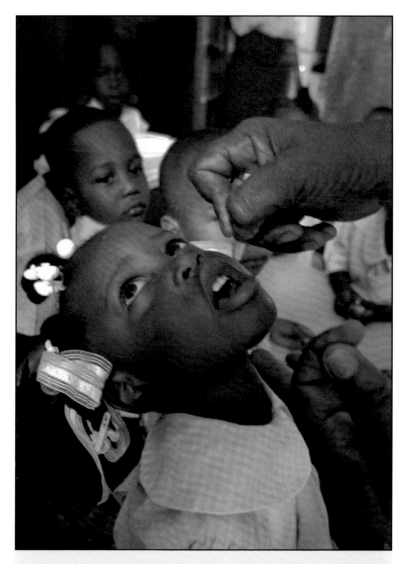

Although Haiti and the Dominican Republic were declared polio free in the 1980s, the immunization rate is still not adequate to prevent outbreaks of new strains. In 2002, Haiti reported 21 cases of polio, including two deaths, and the Dominican Republic had 13 cases. That year, PAHO conducted a nine-week inoculation campaign, and continues to monitor data on polio, typhoid, measles, diphtheria, violence, and acute malnutrition.

all children could be vaccinated. Known as Days of Tranquility, these cease-fires allowed the health teams to travel freely and give children their vaccine. Once, a doctor who went with a team of vaccinators recalled walking through the field on a Day of Tranquility. He was terrified when his group was stopped by guerrilla fighters. The fighters only wanted them to return to a village they had missed and give the medicine to its children. The program was so successful that polio has almost disappeared from the hemisphere. Brief outbreaks in Haiti and the Dominican Republic were quickly identified and controlled. Now, WHO also uses the National Immunization Days and hopes to rid the world of polio.

PAHO's new target is stopping measles. PAHO does all it can with a revolving fund to get vaccines, and it also works on HIV/AIDS and tuberculosis control activities. PAHO has had many successes, but another of its major successes is working with local and national governments. It raises their awareness and gets them to act on health problems.

INTER-AMERICAN CHILDREN'S INSTITUTE

In 1927, an inter-American conference set up the Inter-American Children's Institute (Institución Interamericana de Niño, or IIN, in Spanish) to improve the lives of children. The idea came from Dr. Luis Morquio, a Uruguay pediatrician. He got Uruguay to adopt a Child Code, saying that childhood was a special state and that children needed special protection. In 1919, Dr. Morquio proposed the Inter-American Office for the Protection of Children. His plan was that it would "be the center of studies, action and dissemination [spreading information], in the Americas, of all issues related to children."[22] At first only 10 countries signed the agreement, but all Latin American states became part when the OAS charter was signed.

Up until 1956, the IIN stressed health issues for children. Now, it spends more time on the social, economic, and cultural rights of children, such as improving their daily lives, trying to assure they receive sufficient food, housing, health care, and even education. To accomplish this, the IIN created many departments within its organization. Since Dr. Morquio first proposed special protection for children, other declarations and conventions, like that of the United Nations, have described the rights of children.

INTERNATIONAL CONVENTION ON THE RIGHTS OF THE CHILD

In 1989, the United Nations adopted the International Convention on the Rights of the Child. This document became the standard for children's rights. These include the right to survival, protection, education, health care, and legal and social services. It also calls for being free of abuse and exploitation, hunger, and having the right to take part in family, social, and cultural life. The basic principles maintain respect for the views of the child, nondiscrimination against children, and support for practices that best serve the interest of the child. In the global community, only the United States and Somalia have not signed it, believing it would take away their sovereignty to act as they please. Since the convention was written, two optional protocols (one on child soldiers and one on sexual exploitation) have been added. Although the United States signed these protocols, several countries in the world have refused to do so.

The OAS member states agreed to the UN Convention on the Rights of the Child, and the IIN took on the responsibility to help the countries of the hemisphere comply. The IIN wanted to make sure the states of the Americas had policies and agencies that work for children's needs. It made sample laws so member states could pass legislation to reduce inequality and guarantee child rights. The IIN began with laws against child labor and commercial sexual exploitation (using children as prostitutes or in sexually explicit films or photos) and then added laws to help with drug abuse prevention and disability

Here Colombian soldiers escort a 13-year old rebel of the Revolutionary Armed Forces of Colombia (FARC). Child soldiers have been used by both sides in the conflict to gather intelligence, make and deploy mines, and serve as advance troops in attacks against paramilitaries, soldiers, and police officers. In July 2002, the International Criminal Court drafted a treaty stating that the use of children under the age of 15 in hostilities will be considered a war crime and prosecuted in the court.

It expanded to include laws on how to treat youth offenders (young criminals), adopted children, street children, refugees (escaping political persecution), and child soldiers.

Currently, child soldiers are a major problem in the world, and Colombia has more than any other country in the Americas. Although Colombia signed the protocol against using children to fight, it has failed to ratify it. Human Rights Watch, an organization that monitors human rights abuses, estimated there are more than 11,000 child soldiers in Colombia.[23] Children join fighting forces because they are poor or are kidnapped at gunpoint. They are promised food and money, but at other times, it is a way for them to leave abusive homes. Some are street children who have been abandoned by their parents and have no place to go. In Colombia, fighters have been found as young as 13 years old. On opposite sides in battles, children continue to kill children. The IIN keeps trying to deal with this and other problems regarding children's well-being.

INTER-AMERICAN COMMISSION OF WOMEN

The Inter-American Commission of Women (Comisión Interamericana de Mujeres, or CIM) was established in 1928 primarily by Latin American teachers who wanted to gain equal rights between men and women. Most of these teachers were the first generation of educated women in the hemisphere, and they wanted to gain the same educational, political, economic, and social rights as men. Women had little part in the Pan American Union, but at the PAU meeting in Havana, Cuba, they finally gained recognition with their new institute.

Just as with the General Assembly, the CIM has one delegate from each member state. These delegates meet every two years and work at home with national women's organizations, nongovernmental organizations, and governmental agencies. The CIM has had a major impact on OAS policies. Even before the founding of the OAS, at the meeting in Chapultepec, Mexico, the CIM worked to pass a resolution that called upon all governments to stop discriminating against women. Since the entrance of Caribbean nations into the OAS, Caribbean delegates have joined the CIM and now work in their states on women's concerns. Today, women participate and are represented at every level in the OAS.

By 1960, when all American states allowed women to vote, the CIM had established offices and had partnerships with organizations in each country in the hemisphere. The CIM then focused on bringing equal social and economic rights to women. It strives to guarantee fair wages and safe working conditions for both rural and urban women. Education and training are important so women learn the skills they need to improve their position and opportunities. The CIM works closely on these issues with the UN Commission on the Status of Women, UNESCO (the UN organization to improve the well-being of citizens), and the International Labor Organization.

PAN AMERICAN INSTITUTE OF GEOGRAPHY AND HISTORY

Like CIM, the Pan American Institute of Geography and History (PAIGH) began in 1928. Areas of the hemisphere, such as the dense Amazon jungles and remote mountains, were unexplored. These locations needed to be mapped and to have their natural resources recorded. The PAIGH's headquarters are in Mexico City. From the beginning, it was a scientific organization. It works in the fields of cartography, or mapmaking; geology; history; and geophysics, a kind of earth science. Often, it works with universities and local organizations as well as with international groups.

INTER-AMERICAN INDIAN INSTITUTE

In 1940, a special conference organized the Inter-American Indian Institute (III) to find solutions to the special needs of indigenous peoples. From the time of the conquistadors, when native peoples were often enslaved, racial prejudice has existed. Today, a few tribal peoples live as their people have lived for centuries, but most Indians at least understand the modern world. Many Native Americans have become well-educated professionals, and many have left their lands and gone to cities seeking jobs. Today, there are more than 20 million indigenous peoples in Latin America and the Caribbean. Most live in Guatemala, Ecuador, Bolivia, and Peru, but some no longer identify themselves as Indian peoples. In the beginning, most of the representatives in the III were non-Indian

(continues on page 78)

RIGOBERTA MENCHU TUM: NOBEL PEACE PRIZE WINNER

Rigoberta Menchu Tum was born into a peasant Maya Indian family in the highlands of Guatemala in 1959. She grew up speaking Quiche, the local language, and like the rest of her family she went each day to the fields to work. From the nuns in Catholic schools, she learned to read, write, and speak Spanish. Later, she taught herself other Indian languages.

From the time Menchu had been a baby, a civil war had raged in her homeland, and the military had enforced a violent regime, wiping out whole villages of indigenous peoples. Death squads killed thousands of innocent people who opposed the government. Before she reached age 20, she began working to bring rights to poor peasants and to organize demonstrations against the government. Accused of being guerrillas, her father, mother, two of her brothers, and several nieces and nephews were tortured and killed by the military.

Menchu continued her work for social justice and joined the 31st of January Popular Front, organizing Indians to resist and protest the military oppression. Because of her work, she was forced into hiding and eventually fled to Mexico. She helped establish the Committee for Peasant Unity (CUC) to work against the Guatemalan regime and for human rights. In 1983, Venezuelan-French author Elizabeth Burgos helped Menchu write a book using other Maya's experiences as well as her own to explain the plight of the Indians. Her book is called *I, Rigoberta Menchu*. It gained international attention and brought support for the struggle of indigenous people.

In 1992, she became the youngest person ever awarded the Nobel Peace Prize. The Nobel Committee said it was "in recognition of her work for social justice and ethno-cultural reconciliation

Nobel Peace Prize winner and activist, Rigoberta Menchu

based on respect for the rights of indigenous peoples." She has worked with the United Nations as an official spokesperson for the UN International Decade of Indigenous People from 1994 to 2003, and she helped write the Declaration of the Rights of Indigenous Peoples. When the civil war ended, she did all she could to get those responsible for the mass killings and abuses in Guatemala to stand trail for their crimes against humanity. She has continued working for justice for indigenous peoples, and in 2007, she announced she would run for the presidency of Guatemala.

(continued from page 75)

participants. But starting in 1985, Indian delegates played an increasing part in the institute, and now many groups of indigenous people share in its planning and activities.

In recent times, indigenous peoples have become outspoken about their will to be treated with equality and dignity. Rigoberta Menchu Tum, an Indian of Maya descent and Nobel Peace Prize winner, helped organized the Committee for Peasant Unity to speak out against abuses of indigenous peoples. They want to control their own affairs and have made attempts to get governments to recognize their ancestral lands, languages, traditions, and cultures. The III has responded with reform measures and is creating a Center of Information and Documentation of Indian Peoples of the Americas, where information on all the indigenous peoples can be gathered. Moreover, it has started the Hemispheric Forum of Indigenous Peoples of the Americas. Its purpose is to help establish a conference for continuing discussion of urgently needed intercultural issues. Along with the United Nations and other organizations, the III is writing the American Declaration on the Rights of Indigenous Peoples. This document can serve as a basis for guaranteeing Indians equality and full participation in their countries.

INTER-AMERICAN INSTITUTE FOR COOPERATION ON AGRICULTURE

The last specialized organization under the OAS started as an agricultural commission within the PAU. Today, it is called the Inter-American Institute for Cooperation on Agriculture (IICA). The IICA began in 1942 during World War II to study tropical plants. During the war, Europe lost control over tropical lands in Asia where crops important to the war effort were grown. These were crops such as rubber, rice, tea, and plants used to make medicines. The Allied countries began to look elsewhere for these valuable plants. Two men, U.S. Secretary of Agriculture Henry Wallace and Director General of Agriculture for Ecuador Ernesto Molestina, presented the idea of establishing an institute to research tropical crops in Turrialba, Costa Rica. Their plan was accepted. Although it became a partner to the OAS in 1948, by 1960 only 15 American states were members. Today, all the countries of the hemisphere take part in the IICA.

It set up other separate institutions, such as the Tropical Agriculture Research and Education Center (CATIE) and the Inter-American Board of Agriculture (IABA), to coordinate successful farm practices among OAS members. With offices in 34 countries, it also works on improving trade and communication and finding better ways for farmers to raise crops and livestock. As an organization for agriculture and rural development, the IICA tries to improve life in the rural communities and to eliminate extreme poverty. Two major goals are providing sustainable agriculture and food security.

Rural people need to grow crops that will protect their lands and bring them income as well as food. Indigenous people and other farmers have a great deal of knowledge. But in the global economy, all farmers need to have an understanding of world markets. The IICA helps with this knowledge and at the same time works to assure food security. Food security means providing sufficient food so people in the region do not suffer hunger or malnutrition. If crops that wear out the soil are grown each year, the land will become infertile. If all crops are grown for export to a world market, people may lack the land they need to grow their food. Large plantations or corporations often only grow food for the marketplace, and local people go hungry. Food security means having land, seeds, water, and all needed resources available so citizens can eat enough food to be healthy and secure from hunger.

The six specialized organizations, PAHO, IIN CIM, PAIGH, III, and IICA, have changed with the times. They continue to operate with much independence, though some of their funding comes from the OAS.

The OAS and Human Rights

SOMETIMES HUMAN RIGHTS ABUSES BY GOVERNMENTS ARE called "crimes against humanity." These crimes are usually torture, kidnapping, illegal imprisonment, or murder by government officials and the military. After World War II and the Nazi Holocaust, people around the world thought about what should be essential rights for humanity. Human rights are usually defined as those rights that belong to all people, no matter what their circumstance: poor or rich, black or white, living in a developing country or a major world power. People have certain fundamental rights just because they are human beings. These rights, though, are not limited to civil and political rights, such as those written in the U.S. Bill of Rights. In Latin America, they have always included social and economic rights such as the right to family life or an education.

THE INTER-AMERICAN HUMAN RIGHTS SYSTEM

The first discussion of human rights in the inter-American system began at the Inter-American Conference for Consolidation of Peace at Buenos Aires in 1936. By then, Hitler's Germany had already begun to discriminate against its Jewish population. The delegate from Chile suggested that the American states support "the right of every individual to life, liberty, and the free exercise of his religion, the practice of which does not conflict with public order." He described how ". . . each country was to grant protection of these rights to everyone within its territory, without distinction of race, sex, nationality or religion."[24] At the time, the proposal was rejected. Nonetheless, the diplomats from the American states discussed human rights again in 1938 and then adopted resolutions on women's equality and workers' rights. At the conference in Chapultepec, Mexico, in 1945, the diplomats asked a committee to draft a Declaration of International Rights and Duties of Man. This declaration would list essential human rights. The declaration was the first statement by an international organization describing the human rights of citizens and the duties of a state to protect its citizens. Six months later, with the influence of Latin American leaders, the United Nations adopted the Universal Declaration of Human Rights.

At the meeting in Bogotá, Colombia, when the OAS charter was signed, the American Declaration of the Rights and Duties of Man was adopted as Resolution 30. Moreover, human rights were put into the original charter and are still there. "Social justice and social security are the basis for lasting peace. . . . The American States proclaim the fundamental rights of the individual without distinction as to race, nationality, creed or sex. . . ."[25] As with many OAS principles, though, its member states have often failed to live up to the high ideals stated in the charter.

These photographs show people allegedly murdered or missing by Colombia's security forces and right-wing paramilitary groups. Armed opposition groups and paramilitary in Colombia and other Latin American countries continue to commit serious human rights violations, although these groups agreed to demobilize. In 2007, OAS representatives sent to Colombia to observe the paramilitary demobilization process received death threats.

AMERICAN DECLARATION OF THE RIGHTS AND DUTIES OF MAN

The preamble of the American Declaration of the Rights and Duties of Man stated:

> All men are born free and equal, in dignity and in rights, and, being endowed by nature with reason and conscience, they should conduct themselves as brothers to one another. The fulfillment of duty by each individual is a prerequisite to the rights of all. Rights

and duties are interrelated in every social and political activity of man. While rights exalt [raise] individual liberty, duties express the dignity of that liberty.[26]

The American Declaration had 38 articles, and it also said, "the essential rights of man are not derived from the fact that he is a national [citizen] of a certain state, but are based upon attributes of the human personality."[27] Since the time of Simón Bolívar, American states agreed these rights existed. Most Latin Americans believed just by being born, people deserve these basic rights. These rights include civil and political rights such as life, liberty, personal security, equality before the law, expression, assembly, association, and the right to participate in government. They also include the cultural, economic, and social rights such as the right to health care, education, work with fair wages, leisure time, a private and family life, and protection from unemployment, disability, and old age. Although the American Declaration was accepted, no provision was made for the enforcement of the rights. A few members wanted to include some kind of enforcement in the document, but other states were afraid of losing their sovereignty.

ASSURING RIGHTS: THE INTER-AMERICAN COMMISSION ON HUMAN RIGHTS

The OAS delegates debated how best to assure basic human rights to all peoples of the hemisphere. In 1959, they created the Inter-American Commission on Human Rights (IACHR). At the time, member states failed to reach agreement to set up an inter-American court to deal with abuses. From the beginning, a part of the IACHR's job has been to make citizens aware of human rights and to make recommendations to the OAS. According to the current OAS charter, the IACHR is instructed to "promote the observance and protection of human rights and to serve as consultative organ of the Organization in these matters."[28]

Today, the IACHR is an independent commission and acts for all the member states. Seven commissioners are elected by the General Assembly. It is the duty of those elected to the IACHR to represent all Americans and not just citizens from their own country. In addition to sitting on the commission, each commissioner acts as a judge for particular human rights. These special areas include freedom of expression and fair treatment for detainees and prisoners as well as for migrant workers and their families. The commission recognizes that both the country that has workers leaving and the country that has workers arriving have to deal with the issues of migrant workers. Other special concerns include the rights of women, children, and indigenous peoples, as well as racial discrimination, especially against those of African descent.

The IACHR headquarters are in Washington, D.C., but sometimes it holds meetings in other countries. By 1961, the IACHR began to visit member states to observe any special concerns. Its first tour was to the Dominican Republic. Since then, the IACHR has made visits to 23 member states, checking some states more than once. In 2004, the IACHR sent a fact-finding team to the Caribbean state of Haiti. It believed the government was prosecuting political prisoners rather than true lawbreakers. Democratically elected president Jean-Bertrand Aristide fled the country because of rebel threats on his life. In the new government, Aristide's supporters, rather than rebel leaders who had pushed him out of office, were being held and punished. The rebel chief Louis-Jodel Chamblain was tried and cleared of charges of assassination of a former Aristide supporter. As a result, a delegation of five representatives, led by IACHR Commissioner Clare Roberts from Antigua and Barbuda, traveled to Haiti. This fact-finding team met with a variety of government officials, citizens and legal groups, judges, and UN representatives. Their report criticized the Haitian government's actions. This process of working with other international groups helps to bring more pressure for governments to correct human rights abuses.

In 1965, the IACHR was given the power to look into complaints or petitions from citizens of abuses by their government. Citizens often fail to get justice in their home country. Since then, the IACHR has received thousands of petitions and made recommendations on more than 12,000 cases.

Despite the IACHR reports and recommendations, countries frequently refuse to change their actions. Such an example is Argentina during the Dirty War, when the military took over the government. In the 1970s and 1980s, the military government committed crimes against humanity. U.S. President Jimmy Carter pressured the Argentinean government to allow the IACHR to visit, and in 1979, it agreed. The commission wrote a crushing report on the murderous condition of human rights. The government then threatened to withdraw from the OAS if it were condemned in the General Assembly. As a result of its threats, little action was taken by the OAS.

In addition to looking into special problems that come before it, the IACHR holds public meetings. In Guatemala in 2006, the IACHR called a special meeting and held several public hearings on human rights issues involving Central American countries. These meetings discussed concerns about the property rights of indigenous peoples, treatment of women prisoners in Honduras, the human rights problems of free trade agreements, and the human rights situation of union members in El Salvador. The commission can make recommendations and try to work with individual citizens and member states if they are willing. The commissioners bring the state and the citizens together to find a settlement. Today, if the state refuses to carry out the recommendations, the IACHR can send the case to the Inter-American Court of Human Rights. But until the Inter-American Court was set up, the commission had few means of dealing with violations.

(continues on page 88)

LAS MADRES (THE MOTHERS) OF THE PLAZA DE MAYO

The Dirty War, a violent military overthrow of the government in Argentina in 1976, made crimes against humanity an everyday happening. The military government kidnapped, tortured, and killed those who protested. Most were young people who wanted a return to democracy. Many were pregnant women, and they gave birth in prison. Afterward, they were killed. Their babies, though, were given to military officials to raise as their own.

The families of those who "disappeared" never knew what happened to their children and grandchildren. They searched for family members at police stations, government offices, and military barracks but never found their daughters and sons. The military regime refused to allow any discussion of the missing persons. Mothers wrote letters to the government and military departments, but their letters went unanswered. A few of those who spoke out, disappeared as well.

Azucena Villaflor de Vincenti searched for her sons and her daughter-in-law for six months. While looking for her family, Villaflor met other mothers also seeking their children. She and 13 others decided they must do something to force the government to respond. So on April 30, 1979, they put white scarves on their heads, symbolizing the diapers of their missing children, and went to the Plaza de Mayo. They stood together in front of the Casa Rosa, the presidential palace. Police came and told them it was illegal to stand there. The mothers then went to the pyramid at the center of the plaza and began to walk around it. They met and walked each Thursday afternoon; as the war continued, more mothers joined them. They carried large posters with photos of their loved ones. Before long, the world noticed. The mothers' bravery and nonviolent protest eventually brought them international attention and awards. But they just wanted the return of their family.

Mothers of Plaza de Mayo, marching in Buenos Aires Plaza de Mayo in 1979.

The war ended in 1983 when a civilian government took control of Argentina. The military regime had killed and tortured their opponents and dumped them far out into the ocean or in unmarked graves. By then, between 11,000 and 30,000 people had "disappeared" and were never heard from again.

The government, though, pardoned the officers who had committed human rights abuses. Las Madres and Las Abuelas (The Grandmothers) failed to give up. They wanted to bring the guilty

(continues)

(continued)

parties to justice and to find out about their family. They kept up their nonviolent vigil each Thursday. Las Madres began to work with U.S. scientist Mary-Claire King, who used genetic evidence to match the grandchildren with their biological grandmothers. About 50 such children have been identified, but many, sadly, have little in common with their families, having been raised by war supporters.

In January 2006, Las Madres held their final demonstration; it marked 1,500 times they had walked. This time it was a great celebration, for President Néstor Kirchner suspended the laws that saved military leaders from prosecution. "We are all Mothers of the Plaza de Mayo," he declared.

(continued from page 85)

THE AMERICAN CONVENTION ON HUMAN RIGHTS AND THE INTER-AMERICAN COURT OF HUMAN RIGHTS

By the 1970s, the states were ready to update the American Declaration of the Rights and Duties of Man. They wrote a new agreement called the American Convention on Human Rights. This document held the promise that states were actually required to carry out these rights, within their power to do so. It established a court in San José, Costa Rica. Twenty-five states signed the Pact of San José in 1973, although neither the United States nor Canada has done so, fearing intervention into their domestic affairs. Since the American Convention went into force in the hemisphere, additional protocols have been added. For example, the two protocols have declared the practices of the death penalty and abortion contrary to human rights.

The Inter-American Court of Human Rights was established when the American Convention on Human Rights was signed. In 1978, it went into force and acted as an independent court, hearing evidence and advising on human rights. Seven judges are elected from the member states to sit on the court. It listens to and rules on the cases referred to it by the IACHR as well as cases coming from member states. Individual citizens with complaints must first go to the IACHR to seek help. Governments acting for citizens or for their country may go directly to the court. With the establishment of the Inter-American Court, a second major agency for human rights protection in the Western Hemisphere came into operation.

Many cases have come before the Inter-American Court. One case brought by the Maya Indian survivors of the village of Plan De Sanchez involved the massacre of 128 people by the Guatemalan army in 1982. In 1995, survivors presented testimonies and petitioned the IACHR to find the government troops guilty. Four years later, the IACHR sent the case to the Inter-American Court. In 2004, the Inter-American Court ruled that the Guatemalan state had committed the massacres and genocide (killing of a race or culture). It was the first ruling against the 626 massacres carried out by Guatemalan troops in the 1980s. The court awarded millions of dollars to the relatives of the victims.

The Inter-American Court also gives advice to other OAS agencies. When asked, the court gives opinions to governments on laws and proposed laws and whether they fit within the American Convention on Human Rights. Twenty-one of the 35 member states, though neither the United States nor Cuba, have agreed to follow the rulings of the court.

THE INTER-AMERICAN INSTITUTE OF HUMAN RIGHTS

In 1980, the Inter-American Institute of Human Rights was established as one of the centers for teaching about human rights. It encourages support for human rights as written in the American Convention. According to the Inter-American Institute, its work is "based on principles of representative democracy, the rule of law, ideological pluralism [holding differing opinions or ideas] and respect for fundamental rights and freedom."[29]

Human rights became more important to the global community after World War II. The horrors of genocide practiced by the Nazi government forced the world to deal more actively with the problem. In the years following the war, various world organizations wrote declarations calling for the essential rights of human beings, though Latin America was the first.

Emphasis
on Democratic
Governments

ALTHOUGH MOST KINGS OR QUEENS NO LONGER RULE A country with absolute authority, Latin American dictators have sometimes ruled as if a country were their own kingdom. Some dictators came to power by overthrowing the government using military force. Others grabbed more and more power while in office. When dictators take control, the people lose their rights. In recent times, some dictators have ruled with almost unlimited power. But just as in the U.S. revolution against England in 1776, people have sometimes risen up against abuses of power and established new governments. One example is the Sandinista revolution in Nicaragua that started a rebellion and forced the brutal dictator Anastasio Somoza to flee to the United States in 1979.

From 1936 to 1979, the Somoza family ruled Nicaragua. The Somoza dictatorship looted the economy and committed human rights violations until the government of Anastasio Somoza *(right)* was overthrown in 1979 by the Sandinista regime. He was assassinated in Paraguay by a multinational commando team in 1980.

A DICTATOR IN NICARAGUA

Nicaragua was the first Central American country to be invaded by the United States. It was invaded in 1855, and the marines landed again in 1908. The U.S. military stayed in Nicaragua from 1912 until 1925 and came back in 1926. Many Nicaraguans resented U.S. interference. In the 1930s, U.S. President Franklin Roosevelt declared his "Good Neighbor Policy," and for a time, the United States gave up military invasions into Latin America. Instead, it tried to influence the region in other ways, including training national guards in U.S. military methods. As a result, in 1933, the United States withdrew from Nicaragua, but first it established, trained, and armed the Nicaraguan National Guard. Anastasio Somoza was chosen to command the National Guard. Within three years, Somoza used the armed Guard to take over as dictator of Nicaragua; he murdered Augusto Sandino, who had fought against the U.S Marines.

Somoza and his two sons, first Luis and then Anastasio, ruled with little regard for laws. They schemed to gain wealth. By the 1970s, their family and friends owned much of the land and 26 of the largest businesses. For 40 years, the Somoza family dictatorship reigned with torture, corruption, and brutal force. Most Nicaraguans lived in extreme poverty and longed for a better life. In 1961, a group of students began the Sandinista National Liberation Front (FSLN), named for Sandino, to put an end to the Somoza regime. In Latin America, it was called "la revolución de los muchachos" (the kids' revolution) because students and street youths took part. Even the Roman Catholic Church supported an armed rebellion. In June 1979, the OAS called for Somoza's resignation. When Somoza resigned, the Sandinista revolutionaries took over the government. The Sandinistas became the people's choice and the only military power in Nicaragua. When they came to govern, the Sandinistas set up the five-member Junta of National Reconstruction. One member of the junta, Daniel Ortega Saavedra, had been the military commander of the Sandinistas. Ortega was a self-declared Socialist who believed in social justice for the poor. The first act of the junta was to take over the Somoza family's lands and give them to the poor.

NO TROOPS TO NICARAGUA

Because of this, U.S. President Ronald Reagan believed the Sandinista government was "Communist." He saw the new Sandinista government as a threat to U.S. interests, trade, and influence in Nicaragua. In the OAS General Assembly, the U.S. delegate proposed sending soldiers from various member states into Nicaragua as an OAS force to stop the Sandinistas. For the first time in its history, the OAS showed its independence and voted against a U.S. resolution to invade. Many Latin Americans believed the Sandinistas represented the true will of the citizens. When the Sandinista revolution started, hundreds of young people from Costa Rica, Nicaragua's southern neighbor,

The capture of Eugene Hasenfus, the sole survivor of a cargo plane shot down by the Sandinistas, revealed the involvement to the highest level of the United States in supplying weapons to the Contras, a guerrilla army fighting the Nicaraguan government. Sentenced to 25 years in prison for arms trafficking, he was eventually pardoned and released by Nicaraguan President Daniel Ortega.

had crossed the border to fight with the Sandinistas against the hated Somoza dictatorship.

When the Sandinistas took control, many of Somoza's National Guard fled to neighboring Honduras. There, they formed a guerrilla army known as the Contras. Without OAS approval to send troops to fight the Sandinistas, the United States acted on its own. Within a year, the U.S. military began training the Contra fighters and supplying them with weapons, advisors, and money. With this aid, the Contra guerrillas fought the Sandinistas, while the Sandinista government received arms from Soviet bloc countries. Soon, much of the government's resources went to combating the Contras. The guerrilla war continued for 10 years as the Contras slipped over the border or hid in the Nicaraguan jungles to fight. Both Honduras and Costa Rica suffered from the war, while El Salvador and Guatemala had their own civil wars. Central America was a war zone.

NICARAGUA AND THE PEACE PLAN

The OAS meetings discussed activities of the Sandinistas. Latin Americans believed the revolution in Nicaragua was due to poverty and social injustice and not due to Soviet intervention. But the United States believed otherwise and wanted a military victory. Threatened with the loss of U.S. aid money and financial support for the OAS, it was hard to oppose U.S. policy. Consequently, Latin American leaders met outside the OAS, hoping to find a way to bring peace to Central America. Leaders of Colombia, Mexico, Panama, and Venezuela formed the Contadora Group and the Contadora Support Group of Argentina, Brazil, Peru, and Uruguay. They worked out a peace plan. It called for the withdrawal of all foreign advisors, nonintervention into the affairs of other states, support for pluralistic democracy, and arms limitations. The U.S. government opposed the plan, and the group had difficulty getting its proposal accepted.

(continues on page 98)

ÓSCAR ARIAS SÁNCHEZ: PEACEMAKER

For over a hundred years, wealthy coffee planter families in Costa Rica provided the country's leaders. When Óscar Arias Sánchez was born into one of the richest coffee-growing families on September 13, 1941, his parents may have suspected he would one day lead Costa Rica. But they probably never dreamed he would be the winner of the Nobel Peace Prize. Still, he was elected president twice and won the Nobel Peace Prize in 1987.

Arias grew up on the outskirts of San José in the town of Heredia. In those days, the *cafétaleros*, as the coffee families were called, often worked with their hired hands. During harvest time, they helped pick the coffee beans. The cafétaleros and their workers also celebrated harvest festivals and baptisms together.

When Arias was seven years old, Costa Rica decided to do away with its standing army. He grew up believing his country could count on its diplomacy, instead of an army, to keep peace with its neighbors. When Arias finished high school at Colegio Saint Frances, he went to the United States to study at Boston University. He became interested in economics and returned home to attend the University of Costa Rica; he later went to England to earn a doctorate in political science.

During the 1960s, Arias became active in the socialist National Liberation Party (PLN), and in 1970, he began working for the election of José Figueres to the presidency. When Figueres won two years later, Arias was appointed minister of national planning and political economy. Later, he won a seat in congress and was elected secretary-general of the PLN in 1979 before winning the presidency in 1986.

As president, Arias worked to improve the country's economic condition, education, and health care. His desire for peace in Central America led him to seek a solution to the fighting supported by the

Óscar Arias Sánchez

Cold War superpowers. In his speech before the Nobel Prize committee, Arias said:

> I pay no attention to those. . . unwilling to believe that a lasting peace can be genuinely embraced by those who march under a different ideological banner or those who are more accustomed to cannons of war than to councils of peace.

(continues)

(continued)

> We do not judge, much less condemn, any other nation's political or ideological system, freely chosen. . . . We cannot require sovereign states to conform to patterns of government not of their own choosing.

He then called upon the superpowers to: "Send our people plowshares instead of swords, pruning hooks instead of spears."

With the money Arias received from the prize, he started the Arias Foundation for Peace and Human Progress, to promote peace and equality around the world. Arias has been honored by numerous universities and organizations in the global community.

(continued from page 95)

Meanwhile, Óscar Arias Sánchez was elected president of Costa Rica. He asked all the presidents of Central and South America to come to San José for his inauguration. In his inaugural address, Arias declared nonintervention "to be a sacred right of the nations of the Americas."[30] On that day in 1986, Arias met with nine presidents and spoke of finding peace for the region. He told them that all Central Americans had the right to choose the type of government they wanted and no superpower could impose its will on the people. Arias tried to find a solution to the bloodshed in his country by getting Costa Rica free of the fighting between the Contras and Sandinistas. Arias closed the Contras airstrip that had been operating in his country and had the head of the CIA in Costa Rica arrested.

Soon, Arias gathered four other Central American presidents—from El Salvador, Guatemala, Honduras, and

Nicaragua—to talk about the peace plans the Contadora Group had proposed. The heads-of-state failed to reach agreement, but the next year Arias tried again, proposing his own plan. "Only democracy can end wars between brothers," he once said.[31] He asked the presidents to agree to hold democratic elections and find ways to end the fighting in their countries. Later he said, "We seek in Central America not peace alone, not peace to be followed someday by political progress, but peace and democracy, together, indivisible, an end to the shedding of human blood, which is inseparable from an end to the suppression of human rights."[32]

In August 1987, the five Central American presidents met to sign an agreement based on President Arias's plan. The plan called for a cease-fire in Nicaragua, Guatemala, and El Salvador. The agreement granted amnesty, or pardons, to all guerrilla fighters and called for the release of prisoners jailed for their political beliefs. More meetings and more accords followed, and President Daniel Ortega of Nicaragua, along with the other Central American presidents, agreed to hold free elections, to respect human rights, and to give guerrilla fighters amnesty. Honduras promised to work with both the OAS and with UN advisors to demobilize, or disband, the Contra guerrillas. This meant the Contras could take part in the national election and return to Nicaraguan life without penalty. For his efforts to bring peace to the region, Arias was awarded the Nobel Peace Prize in 1987.

When Arias received the prize, he said he was grateful because the Nobel committee had "decided to encourage the efforts to secure peace in Central America." He added:

> Peace is not a matter of prizes or trophies. It is not the product of a victory or command. It has no finishing line, no final deadline, no fixed definition of achievement.
>
> Peace is the never-ending process, the work of many decisions by many people in many countries. It is an

attitude, a way of life, a way of solving problems and resolving conflicts. It cannot be forced on the smallest nation or enforced by the largest. It cannot ignore our differences or overlook our common interests. It requires us to work and live together.[33]

ELECTION MONITORING

As President Arias had said, it took many people from many countries and a continuing process to gain peace in Central America. In 1988, the OAS accepted the peace plan. When Nicaraguan President Ortega signed the peace accords, he agreed to a presidential election in February 1990. Before holding elections, though, a cease-fire had to take place. After that, preparation for a secret ballot election could begin. A temporary cease-fire between the Sandinistas and Contras began, and OAS Secretary-General João Clemente Baena Soares agreed to help.

In order to hold elections that were free and fair, President Ortega allowed international observers into the country. Nicaraguan Foreign Minister Miguel D'Escoto Brockmann asked the OAS to send observers, and Secretary-General Soares consented. The OAS then reached two agreements with the Nicaraguan government: One gave privileges to international observers, and the other set up a process with the Supreme Electoral Council of Nicaragua. In the past, the OAS had sent small groups of people into countries, but this was the first time the OAS sent a large team to supervise an election. The team started six months before the election and continued for several weeks after. They were given complete freedom to do their jobs. A Council of the Freely Elected Heads of Governments headed by former U.S. President Jimmy Carter also came to help. The United Nations, too, sent observers. These observer missions worked together on a wide range of tasks. They dealt with the government to change elections rules, help with voter registration, watch polling places on election day, and tally votes. They also worked with the Supreme Electoral Council to prevent

Former U.S. President Jimmy Carter *(far right)* poses for pictures with OAS election observers in Managua, Nicaragua, in 2006. Hundreds of observers from the Carter Center, the OAS, and the European Union were on hand to observe the vote. According to OAS head José Miguel Insulza, the presidential vote, which was won by Daniel Ortega, took place within the law.

violence and with newspapers, radio, and TV stations to provide equal coverage for candidates.

Voter registration took place on four Sundays in October 1989, and 89 percent of Nicaraguans registered. OAS teams went into villages and helped local leaders to assure peaceful and orderly registration. The missions worked with political party leaders and election officials to prepare for the February election. Two candidates, President Ortega of the Sandinistas and Violeta Barrios de Chamorro of the National Opposition Union (UNO) party, led in the surveys. To everyone's surprise, on February 25 when the votes were counted, Chamorro had won. The observers declared the election fair and free from corruption. The practices and procedures established by the observers proved so successful in Nicaragua, they became a model for future OAS missions. By 1991, the OAS had also monitored elections in Guatemala, El Salvador, Panama, Paraguay, Suriname, and Haiti.

SOLDIERS RETURN TO CIVILIAN LIFE

Parts of the preelection agreements in Nicaragua were for demobilizing the Contra fighters and returning them to civilian life. This process was to have begun during the preelection campaigning, but the Contras refused to lay down their arms until after the election. The OAS and the United Nations again established teams of people to help. The International Support and Verification Commission (CIAV) eventually run by the OAS and the UN Observers Group in Central America (OUNCA) filled different roles. The OUNCA was to make sure military aid to the Contras stopped, the territory used by them in Honduras was cleared, and the ex-soldiers were returned to Nicaragua. It checked the cease-fire and kept the two sides separated as the fighters returned to Nicaragua. The OUNCA collected weapons and uniforms and gave the ex-soldiers demobilization certificates. They were then taken to "safe zones" inside Nicaragua. These locations became places where the ex-soldiers received help. In these safe zones, the CIAV helped with resettlement by providing temporary housing, clothing, and food.

The CIAV assisted with a variety of tasks needed to get ex-soldiers back into society. About 60 percent of the ex-soldiers were less than 25 years old, and some were as young as 12 years old. Other ex-soldiers had begun fighting at an early age and had only known a life of war. As a consequence, they had never gone to school or learned a trade. Women and children came to these safe zones, too. Some women had been soldiers, but others were the wives of soldiers. The civil war disabled many soldiers on both sides. It was a challenge to provide for all the needs of the people living in the safe zones.

The United States, Canada, Japan, European countries, and international nongovernmental organizations agreed to give money for humanitarian relief. OAS workers helped to deliver that aid. They gave out tools, cooking utensils, medicine, and bags of beans and rice; they provided training for job skills; and they administered health exams. Often, though, the money needed to provide these items was slow in coming. While waiting for aid in the safe zones, many ex-soldiers got discouraged. They left to make their own way. Sometimes, they had kept their guns, believing they could sell them or use them for protection. Many remained in the hands of civilians. As a result, in the years after the war, Nicaragua saw much violence. Sometimes, groups of bandits roamed the countryside living a life of crime and destruction. Ten years of fighting had left most Nicaraguans living in poverty, and despite free elections and the return to peace, most of the people in Nicaragua remain poor to this day.

UNIT FOR THE PROMOTION OF DEMOCRACY

The OAS had been so successful in Nicaragua, the General Assembly decided to establish the Unit for the Promotion of Democracy (UPD). It further developed a process for observing elections, and since the 1990 Nicaraguan election, this UPD has monitored elections in almost half of the OAS member countries. It returned to Nicaragua to observe other elections, including the 2006 vote when Daniel Ortega was again elected to the presidency.

The UPD also gives services to promote the growth of democracy in the Americas by helping governments strengthen their institutions. It provides education about democracy, though some of its educational programs have been criticized for being too narrow in their understanding of democracy.

As Venezuelan Foreign Minister Ali Rodriguez said at a recent OAS meeting, "Democracy can thrive in many forms as long as those forms honor universal principles such as freedom of speech and respect for human rights."[34] Since the OAS has placed more emphasis on democracy, no totalitarian governments or dictators have come to power in the hemisphere. Still, 14 elected governments have fallen in the years since 1989. In countries without a long democratic tradition, problems remain. As historian Peter Winn said:

> Since 1985, nearly every country has chosen consecutive rulers in democratic elections. In South America where only two countries were ruled by democratically elected presidents in 1979, all had the chief executives chosen at the ballot box in 2004.
>
> Political life is more open, the press and media are more free and local and regional politics are more vibrant. Ethnic and racial minorities, as well as indigenous majorities in Guatemala and Bolivia, are playing more active and influential roles in public life—important steps toward addressing the social subordination [inferiority] that has been among the region's heaviest colonial legacies. . . .
>
> The spread of democracy is clear, but the *quality* of that democracy is more debatable. . . . Political parties, legislatures and judicial systems remain weak, with corruption and impunity [escape from punishment] serious problems in much of the region.[35]

In addition to the problems democracies face from corruption, democratically elected governments have failed to improve the living conditions for the poor. As Foreign Minister Rodriguez said, "The quality of life is simply nonexistent and as a result the quality of democracy is simply precarious and its strength uncertain. Democracy and poverty are simply incompatible."[36]

The OAS:
Successes
and Criticisms

THE OAS IS THE OLDEST REGIONAL ORGANIZATION IN THE hemisphere, though its ideas of union go back to the great liberator, Simón Bolívar. During the first half of the twentieth century, the Pan American Union brought together countries in the hemisphere in the hopes of cooperating on common concerns and security. The American states held conferences, set up inter-American organizations, and signed treaties. After World War II, the need for increased security in the hemisphere seemed essential. The Latin American states and the United States agreed to new treaties to protect them from intervention, to maintain the sovereignty of each state, and to assure nonrecognition of any territory taken by force.

GOOD FAITH SHALL GOVERN
THE RELATIONS BETWEEN STATES

With the signing of the OAS charter in 1948, the American states set down their best model for unity in the hemisphere. They wanted to work together to improve peace, security, democracy, human rights, prosperity, and equality. They wanted to find political, economic, and legal solutions to problems that arose among them. According to the charter: "Good faith shall govern the relations between States."[37] Despite their hopes and desires for good faith relations, over the years the OAS disappointed many Latin American and Caribbean countries. They found their union dominated or at times ignored by the powerful United States. As the first secretary-general, Lleras had warned that the OAS could be only as high-minded as the political will of it members. Still, as the oldest organization in the hemisphere, the OAS seems the best place for countries to find ways to work together. As historian O. Carlos Stoetzer said:

> The OAS is thus in a unique position to solve conflicts and controversies whenever the will to do so is evident. In cases where the United States wanted its own solutions ([as in] Central America), favored extra-continental powers [England over Argentina, as in the Falklands War] Malvinas issue], or decided to turn the clock backwards. . . [invaded Panama in 1989], there is nothing that either the OAS, or the Latin American members through their own efforts, can do.[38]

Because there seemed little Americans could do against the Colossus of the North, they began to establish new subregional organizations to fulfill some of their needs. The Contradora Group and Costa Rican president Arias launched a peace plan for Central America, despite U.S. objections. CARICOM, MERCOSUR, and other alliances developed trading blocs and

In 1997 at the 13th MERCOSUR Summit in Montevideo, Uruguay, the MERCOSUR member countries and associate members made a commitment to strengthen the process of political, financial, social, cultural, and scientific integration among Latin American nations. Pictured are presidents Eduardo Frei of Chile, Juan Carlos Wasmosy of Paraguay, Carlos Menem of Argentina, Julio Maria Sanguinetti of Uruguay, Fernando Henrique Cardoso of Brazil, and Hugo Banzer of Bolivia.

then began to work toward more political unity among the states. For example, when the OAS was too slow to respond to crises in Paraguay in 1996 and 1999, MERCOSUR stepped in to resolve the problems. These associations have improved the cooperation among hemisphere states outside the OAS. Nonetheless, individual states remain active members of the OAS and take part in its wide-ranging projects and operations.

The United States remains one of the most powerful nations in the world, and in the past, it has bent the OAS to its will. Recent events within the organization, though, hold the promise that a new pattern may be emerging. Latin American countries are showing more independence inside the OAS. This may be the result of more elected socialist or social democratic governments coming to power in the hemisphere.

The election of José Miguel Insulza to the office of secretary-general in 2005 was the first time a U.S.-backed candidate failed to win that office. Another example was the refusal of the General Assembly in 2003 to elect Rafael E. Martinez, the U.S. candidate, to a seat on the seven-member Inter-American Commission of Human Rights. This was the first time in its existence that the IACHR has been without a U.S. representative. The OAS continues to monitor elections in the hemisphere. And it verified the democratic election of President Hugo Chávez of Venezuela in 2004, despite the opposition of U.S. President George W. Bush.

THE OAS CHANGES WITH THE GLOBAL COMMUNITY

The OAS has proved itself capable of reform. As the needs of the hemisphere changed, it updated its charter. Over the years, the OAS has demonstrated its ability to grow in new directions. Since monitoring elections in Nicaragua, the OAS missions have given major support to continuing peaceful and democratic elections in the hemisphere. At times, the OAS has moved against undemocratic practices of member governments. Resolution 1080 and charter changes provided greater protection to democratic governments against seizures of power by dictators. Most recently in 1993, through the efforts of the OAS, Guatemalan President Jorge Serrano was unable to assume dictatorial power. These are major political successes for the OAS and its ability to turn words into actions.

The OAS has attempted to strengthen democracy by working with both local governments and national legislatures. Because corruption is a major problem, the OAS has helped some countries fight against corrupt officials as it encourages the rule of law. Its emphasis on human rights with the establishment of the IAHRC and the Inter-American Human Rights Court has helped in exposing and dealing with human rights abuses in the hemisphere.

Several programs sponsored by the OAS have brought a better life to many peoples in the hemisphere—from security to democracy, human rights, and health care. The OAS has been the major coordinator in the removal of land mines in the Americas and has provided help with natural disasters. Its six specialized organizations have improved health standards; gained rights for women, children, and indigenous peoples; and promoted agriculture and sustainable development. Moreover, its technical advice and its ability to partner with other organizations and groups have benefited the peoples of the Americas.

ECONOMIC GROWTH FAILS TO END POVERTY

The developing countries of the Americas, though, still face major problems. Despite the CIDI and the AICD (OAS agencies designed to help with economic growth and well-being) widespread poverty remains. The growth of member states' economies has been irregular, and the benefits have usually been shared only by the wealthy and upper middle class. The unequal distribution of incomes, wealth, and land in Latin America remains the largest in the global community. The gap between the many poor and the few rich is huge. According to Winn, "It is a region where only 10 percent of the income goes to the poorest 40 percent of the population, while the wealthiest 20 percent receives almost 60 percent. Moreover, this inequality has *increased* since 1990. . . ."[39]

Forty percent of the people remain in extreme poverty, and many continue to live without hope. While the policies of major lending and development institutions such as the International Monetary Fund (IMF) and World Bank are blamed for most of these economic problems, the OAS has failed to find other successful approaches. The poor of the region saw social and government programs, which acted as their safety net, disappear

Although the economies of many Latin American countries have experienced a high rate of growth, 40 percent of the people remain in extreme poverty. Latin American governments hope to follow the positive example of Chile, which has cut extreme poverty by 65 percent since 1990, and continues to help poor people buy housing, while investing in rural primary education. Yet, similar programs in other countries cannot be of much help if corruption by its leaders is not reduced.

under the policies of the IMF. As winner of the 2001 Nobel Prize in Economics, Joseph E. Stiglitz said:

> In Latin America, growth has not been accompanied by a reduction in inequality, or even in poverty. In some cases poverty has actually increased as evidenced by the urban slums that dot the landscape. The IMF talks with pride about the progress Latin America has made

in market reforms. . . , but has said less about the num-
bers in poverty. [40]

The reason Latin American countries backed away from
the FTAA was because they feared the kinds of trade policies
that benefit the United States at their expense. While the charter of the OAS and many OAS resolutions and documents, such
as the Inter-American Democratic Charter, state the importance of economic improvement for democracy, many people
struggle in poverty. Words and promises, no matter how well
intended, mean little without the deeds and policies necessary
to carry them out.

Although the OAS provides the best forum for hemispheric
cooperation, as the global community continues to change, it
must meet the challenges of the twenty-first century. On the
50th anniversary of the OAS in 1998, Assistant Secretary-
General Christopher Thomas wrote:

> Globalization. . . requires management of change,
> security engagement, sustainable development, multi-
> lateralism and functional interdependence [a workable
> dependence on each other]. How the OAS responds to
> these phenomena related to globalization will deter-
> mine its success. . . and its ability to assume. . . leader-
> ship functions into the twenty-first century.[41]

As globalization brings the countries of the world in closer
contact with each other, they become more interdependent.
They are forced to rely on each other. In the global community,
the OAS has brought the Americas together to work cooperatively. The ability to deal with hemisphere problems through
the organization has helped all countries in the hemisphere.
With better cooperation, more "good faith" relations among the
states, and more deeds that reflect its principles, the OAS can
turn more of its high-minded goals into realities.

CHRONOLOGY

1826   Simón Bolívar calls the Congress of Panama to form a union of American states.

1889–1980   The First International Conference of American States meets and later establishes the Pan American Union.

1902   International Sanitary Bureau founded; today called the Pan American Health Organization (PAHO).

1927   Inter-American Children's Institution (IIN) started.

1928   Inter-American Commission of Women (CIM) and Pan American Institute of Geography and History (PAIGH) established.

1933   American states sign the Convention on the Rights and Duties of States.

1940   Inter-American Indian Institute (III) formed.

1944   Inter-American Institute of Agricultural Sciences formed; today called the Inter-American Institute for Cooperation on Agriculture (IICA).

1945   The Act of Chapultepec pledges to deal with threats of aggression against American republics.

1947   The Inter-American Treaty of Reciprocal Assistance (Rio Treaty) established to assist each other and defend the hemisphere from invasion.

1948   The OAS is established with the signing of the charter, the Pact of Bogotá and the American Declaration of Rights and Duties of Man.

1959   Inter-American Commission on Human Rights (IACHR) established.

1962   Cuba excluded from OAS activities.

1967   Protocol of Buenos Aires created General Assembly and the Permanent Council, established in 1970.

1969   Inter-American Convention on Human Rights signed (ratified in 1973).

1973   CARICOM formed.

1978–1979   Inter-American Court of Human Rights established at San José, Costa Rica.

1985   Protocol Cartagena de Indias gives secretary-general and Permanent Council power to assemble countries with disagreements.

1989–1990   OAS monitors election in Nicaragua.

1991   General Assembly passes Resolution 1080 authorizing a meeting if an elected government is overthrown or suspended.

1992   Protocol of Washington includes more protection of human rights and undemocratic actions by American states (ratified in 1997).

1993   Protocol of Managua strengthens commitment to economic development with Inter-American Council for Integral Development (CIDI/IACID established in 1996).

1994   First Summit of the Americas gathers heads-of-states to discuss hemisphere future.

1995   Treaty of Asunción signed to set up Common Market of the South (MERCOSUR).

2001   Inter American Democratic Charter defines democracy in the Americas.

NOTES

Introduction

1. Nancy San Martin, "A Legacy of Latin America's Wars," *Miami Herald* , February 20, 2005.
2. Ibid.
3. "OAS Helping to Restore Lost Childhood to Young Nicaraguan Landmine Victims," Organization of American States. Available online at *http://www.oas.org/OASpage/ press-releases/press-release.asp?sCodigo=E-143/06.*

Chapter 1

4. Christopher R. Thomas, *The OAS in Its 50th Year: Overview of a Regional Commitment.* Washington, D.C.: OAS, 1998, pp. 4–5.
5. O. Carlos Stoetzer, *The Organization of American States: An Introduction*, 1st ed. New York: Frederick A. Praeger, 1965, p. 118.
6. "Charter of the OAS," The Organization of American States. Available online at *http://www.oas.org/juridico/ english/charter.html.*
7. "Permanent Observers," The Organization of American States. Available online at *http://der.oas.org/permanent _observers.html.*
8. Carlos Andres Perez, "OAS Opportunities," *Foreign Policy* 80, no. 4 (Fall 1990): p. 52.

Chapter 2

9. Alonso Aguilar, *Pan-Americanism from Monroe to the Present: A View from the Other Side.* Revised English edition. New York: Monthly Review Press, 1986, p. 25.
10. Ibid., p. 39.
11. O. Carlos Stoetzer, *The Organization of American States.* 2nd ed. Westport, Conn.: Praeger, 1993, p. 78.

12.   Ibid., p. 142.

13.   Margaret M. Ball, *The OAS in Transition*. Durham, N.C.: Duke University Press, 1969, p. 41.

Chapter 3

14.   "OAS Reiterates Offer to Recover Bodies of Deceased Colombian Lawmakers," Organization of American States. Available online at *http://www.oas.org/OASpage/ press_releases/press_ releases/asp?sCodgio=E-167/07*.

15.   "OAS," U.S. Department of State. Available online at *http://www.state.gov/p/wha/rls/fs/2005/47198.htm*.

16.   "The Inter-American Democratic Charter," University of Minnesota Human Rights Library. Available online at *http://www1.umn.edu/humanrts/oasinstr/cemcharter _2001.html*.

17.   Andres Oppenheimer, "Hemispheric Democratic Charter Will Contain Big Loopholes," *Miami Herald*, September 2, 2001, p. A16.

18.   "Combating Corruption," Organization of American States. Available online at *http://www.oas.org.key%5 fissues/eng/KeyIssue-Detail.asp?kis-sec=7*.

Chapter 4

19.   "Remarks at a Reception for Heads of State at the Summit of the Americas in Miami—Bill Clinton Speech—Transcript," Weekly Compilation of Presidential Documents. Available online at *http://findarticles. com/p/articles/mi-m2889/is-n50-v30/ai-16574943/print*.

Chapter 5

20.   "Whatever Happened to Polio?" Smithsonian National Museum of American History/Behring Center. Available

online at *http://americanhistory.si.edu/polio/poliotoday/expanded.htm*.

21.   Stoetzer, *The Organization of American States*, p. 102.

22.   "History of the Inter-American Children's Institute," Inter-American Children's Institute. Available online at *http://www.iin.oea.org/2005/Historia_del_IIN_ingles.htm*.

23.   "Child Soldiers," Human Rights Watch. Available online at *http://hrw.org/campaigns/crp/index.htm*.

Chapter 6

24.   Ball, *OAS in Transition*, pp. 502–503.

25.   "The OAS Charter," Organization of American States. Available online at *http://www.oas.org/English.charter.html*.

26.   "American Declaration of the Rights and Duties of Man," Organization of American States, Basic Documents. Available online at *http://www/cidh.org/Basicos/basic2htm*.

27.   Ibid.

28.   "Charter of the OAS."

29.   "About US," Inter-American Institute of Human Rights, San José, Costa Rica. Available online at *http://www.iidh.ed.cr/acerca_cont_eng.htm*.

Chapter 7

30.   Peter Winn, *Americas: The Changing Face of Latin America and the Caribbean*, 3rd ed. Berkeley: University of California Press, 2006, p. 550.

31.   Ibid., p. 553.

32.   "Arias Talk on Getting the Nobel," *New York Times*, December 11, 1987, p. A3.

33.   Ibid.

34.   Nancy San Martin and Pablo Bachelet, "Bush Touts Trade, but U.S. Bid to Empower OAS Stalls," *Miami Herald*, June 7, 2005.

35.   Winn, *Americas*, p. 638.

36.   Martin and Bachelet, "Bush Touts Trade."

Chapter 8

37.   "The Charter of the OAS," p. 3.

38.   Stoetzer, *The Organization of American States*. 2nd ed., pp. 270–271.

39.   Winn, *Americas*, p. 635.

40.   Joseph E. Stiglitz, *Globalization and Its Discontents*. New York: W.W. Norton, 2002, p. 79.

41.   Thomas, *The OAS*, p. 81.

BIBLIOGRAPHY

Aguilar, Alonso. *Pan-Americanism from Monroe to the Present: A View from the Other Side*. Revised English edition. New York: Monthly Review Press, 1986.

Ball, M. Margaret. *The OAS in Transition*. Durham, N.C.: Duke University Press, 1969.

Bryan, Anthony T., and Andres Serbin, eds. *Distant Cousins: The Caribbean-Latin American Relationship*. Coral Gables, Fla.: North-South Center Press, 1966.

Chomsky, Noam. *Hegemony or Survival: America's Quest for Global Dominance*. New York: Henry Holt, 2003.

Cooper, Andrew F., and Thomas Legler. "The OAS Democratic Solidarity Paradigm: Questions of Collective and National Leadership." *Latin American Politics and Society* 43, no. 1 (Spring 2001): 103–126.

Dreier, John C. *The Organization of American States and the Hemisphere Crisis*. New York: Harper & Row, 1962.

Farer, Tom, ed. *Beyond Sovereignty: Collectively Defending Democracy in the Americas*. Baltimore: Johns Hopkins University Press.

Foster, Lynn V. *A Brief History of Central America*. New York: Facts On File, 2000.

Grandin, Greg. *Empire's Workshop: Latin America, the United States, and the Rise of the New Imperialism*. New York: Henry Holt, 2006.

Han, Henry H. *Problems and Prospects of the Organization of American States: Perceptions of the Member States' Leaders*. New York: Peter Lang, 1987.

Millett, Richard L. "Beyond Sovereignty: International Efforts to Support Latin American Democracy." *Journal of Inter-American Studies and World Affairs* 36, no. 3 (Fall 1994): 1–23.

Munoz, Heraldo. "The Right to Democracy in the Americas." *Journal of Inter-American Studies and World Affairs* 4, no. 1 (Spring 1998): 1–18.

Perez, Carlos Andres. "OAS Opportunities." *Foreign Policy* 80, no. 4 (Fall 1990): 52–55.

Petras, James, and Steve Vieux. "The Transition to Authoritarian Electoral Regimes in Latin America." *Latin American Perspectives* 21, no. 4 (Fall 1994): 5–20.

Scheman, L. Ronald. *The Inter-American Dilemma: The Search for Inter-American Cooperation at the Centennial of the Inter-American System*. New York: Praeger, 1988.

———. "Rhetoric and Reality: The Inter-American System's Second Century." *Journal of Inter-American Studies and World Affairs* 29, no. 3 (Fall 1987): 1–32.

Sheinin, David. *The Organization of American States*. International Organizations Series, vol. 11. New Brunswick, N.J.: Transaction Publishers Rutgers University, 1996.

Slater, Jerome. *The OAS and United States Foreign Policy*. Columbus, O.H.: Ohio State University Press, 1967.

Stiglitz, Joseph E. *Globalization and Its Discontents*. New York: W.W. Norton, 2002.

Stoessinger, John G. *The Might of Nations: World Politics in Our Time*. 8th ed. New York: Random House, 1986.

Stoetzer, O. Carlos. *The Organization of American States*. 2nd ed. Westport, Conn.: Praeger, 1993.

———. *The Organization of American States: An Introduction*. New York: Praeger, 1965.

Thomas, Christopher R. *The OAS in Its 50th Year: Overview of a Regional Commitment*. Washington, D.C.: OAS INTER-AMER, series no. 65, 1998.

Winn, Peter. *Americas: The Changing Face of Latin America and the Caribbean*. 3rd ed. Berkeley: University of California Press, 2006.

Woodward, Ralph Lee, Jr. *Central America: A Nation Divided*. 2nd ed. New York: Oxford University Press, 1999.

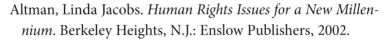

FURTHER READING

Altman, Linda Jacobs. *Human Rights Issues for a New Millennium*. Berkeley Heights, N.J.: Enslow Publishers, 2002.

Kronenwetter, Michael. *Taking a Stand Against Human Rights Abuses*. New York: Franklin Watts, 1990.

Mason, Paul. *Planet Under Pressure: Poverty*. Chicago: Heinemann Library, 2006.

Miller, Debra A. *Nicaragua*. New Haven, Conn.: Lucent Books, 2005.

Pascoe, Elaine. *Neighbors at Odds: U.S. Policy in Latin America*. New York: Franklin Watts, 1990.

WEB SITES

Bogota Conference of American States,
    Charter of the Organization of American States 1948
    http://www.yale.edu/lawweb.avalon/decade/decad062.htm

Common Market of the South (MERCOSUR)
    http://www.mre.gov.br

Council on Hemispheric Affairs
    http://www.coha.org

Human Rights Watch
    http.//www.hrw.org

International Peacemaking and Human Rights Programs
    http://cartercenter.org/countries/Nicaragua.html

Organization of American States
    http://www.oas.org

Summit of the Americas
    http://www.summit-americas.org

United Nations
  http://www.un.org/OAS

The United States and the
  Organization of American States
  http://www.state.gov/p/wha/rt/oas

World Policy Institute:
  Project for Global Democracy and Human Rights
  http://www.worldpolicy.org/globalrights

PICTURE CREDITS

INDEX

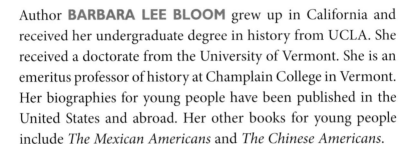

Author **BARBARA LEE BLOOM** grew up in California and received her undergraduate degree in history from UCLA. She received a doctorate from the University of Vermont. She is an emeritus professor of history at Champlain College in Vermont. Her biographies for young people have been published in the United States and abroad. Her other books for young people include *The Mexican Americans* and *The Chinese Americans*.

Series editor **PEGGY KAHN** is a professor of political science at the University of Michigan-Flint. She teaches world and European politics. She has been a social studies volunteer in the Ann Arbor, Michigan, public schools, and she helps prepare college students to become teachers. She has a Ph.D. in political science from the University of California, Berkeley, and a B.A. in history and government from Oberlin College.